from

MW01121978

come to me

nurturing the spiritual birth of your child

Brian E. Hill

Authentic
MEDIA

Authentic Media
We welcome your comments and questions.
129 Mobilization Drive, Waynesboro, GA 30830 USA authenticusa@stl.org
and 9 Holdom Avenue, Bletchley, Milton Keynes, Bucks, MK1 1QR, UK
www.authenticbooks.com

If you would like a copy of our current catalog, contact us at:
1-8MORE-BOOKS
ordersusa@stl.org

Come To Me
ISBN: 1-932805-04-4

Copyright © 2004 by Brian E. Hill

09 08 07 06 05   6 5 4 3 2 1

Published in 2005 by Authentic Media
All rights reserved. No part of this book may be reproduced in any form
without permission in writing from the publisher, except in the case of brief
quotations embodied in critical articles or reviews.

All Scripture quotations, unless otherwise indicated, are taken from the HOLY
BIBLE, NEW INTERNATIONAL VERSION®. NIV®. Copyright ©1973,
1978, 1984 by International Bible Society. Used by permission of Zondervan.
All rights reserved.

Scripture quotations marked NLT are taken from the *Holy Bible*, New Living
Translation, copyright © 1966. Used by permission of Tyndale House
Publishers, Inc., Wheaton, Illinois 60189. All rights reserved.

Library of Congress Cataloging-in-Publication Data available

Cover design: Paul Lewis
Interior design: Angela Duerksen
Editorial team: Carol Pitts, Karen James, and Betsy Weinrich

Printed in the United States of America

DEDICATIONS

This book is dedicated to all of the young parents I have had the privilege to serve over the years and to the wise senior adults who have taught me so much as a parent.

I would also like to dedicate this book to the best wife and mother in the whole world. Keli, I love you and am thankful to God for putting you in my life.

Finally, I dedicate this book to George and Doris Hill—two people who sowed spiritual seeds in my life. Without them I would not be where I am today.

Contents

Introduction

All Christian parents look forward to the day when their son or daughter will commit his or her life to following Jesus. We want our children to have the same faith that we have and hold the same values that we hold. We want them to know God as we know him. Many parents, however, underestimate the significance of getting an early start on introducing their child to his or her Creator.

Sharing the gospel with our children while they are in the formative years of life is crucial. Parents should readily understand that the time to pass on our spiritual beliefs to our children is while they are absorbing information about their world and acquiring convictions about how they view the world in which they live. We must reach them while they are forming their spiritual beliefs, and not after the fact. According to a study done by the North American Mission Board of the Southern Baptist Convention, conversion to Christianity becomes less likely in a person's life after age twelve. Seventy-five percent of conversions to Christianity occur at age twenty and younger.[1] As a person ages, he or she becomes less likely to be baptized and join a local church. Since the most critical time for spiritual development is between the ages of seven and sixteen, one can easily see the importance of presenting the gospel to our children while they are forming their spiritual beliefs.

Evangelism with children is a process—not a one-time event. Bringing a child to the point of deciding to follow Jesus begins in the home long before the day he makes a profession of faith. Our approach to the spiritual training of our children should be as deliberate and intentional as our approach to their school education. No parent would expect his or her child to skip kindergarten through the twelfth grade and go straight to graduation. Neither would it be reasonable to allow our children to skip years of spiritual development and instruction, expecting them suddenly to become a disciple of Christ! Evangelizing our children requires a long-term commitment and a desire to nurture their spiritual beliefs.

Perhaps surprisingly, parents very often feel ill-prepared to bring their children to the point of making a decision to follow Jesus for the rest of their lives. Many parents depend on the pastor of a church to lead their children to Christ. But it is my conviction that this is an honor and a privilege that belongs to the parent. The church cannot take the place of the parents, but rather should *partner* with them to lead their children to Christ. The purpose of this book is to equip and enable both parents and churches alike to become more effective in the area of evangelism with children.

On many occasions parents have asked me, as a pastor, how they can know their child is ready to be saved. This book will not only help parents to know when their child is ready and equip them to deal with their child when they are ready, but it will also help mother and father in the discipleship process.

Christians are called to make disciples, and Christian parents are called to make disciples of their children—a process that begins in the nursery and continues to the day they possess an authentic relationship with God through his son, Jesus Christ. In this book we will examine some proactive steps parents and Christian educators can take in the process of turning children into lifelong disciples of Jesus. Parents, the first nine chapters are for you, to help you pass on your spiritual beliefs to your children. The final chapter is written for you to share with your child. It is a gospel presentation you can use to lead your child to make a faith commitment to Christ.

May God bless moms and dads, sons and daughters, as they explore the pages of this book.

Chapter One
The Heart of Jesus for Children

People were also bringing babies to Jesus to have him touch them. When the disciples saw this, they rebuked them. But Jesus called the children to him and said, "Let the little children come to me, and do not hinder them, for the kingdom of God belongs to such as these. I tell you the truth; anyone who will not receive the kingdom of God like a little child will never enter it. (Luke 18:15–17)

Jesus Loves the Little Children

The eighteenth chapter of the gospel of Luke contains a story about parents bringing their children to Jesus. Like many of us, these parents wanted to introduce their children to Jesus. They wanted Jesus to touch their children and to bless them. He was more than willing to accommodate that desire because Jesus loves children. His desire for our children today is the same as it was in Luke chapter eighteen—our Lord wants children to have a personal relationship with him. As Jesus traveled and ministered throughout Israel, the people saw him as someone who, above all, loved their children. How outstanding it is to know that Jesus loves our children even more than we do! Moms and dads today need to understand that the Lord wants them to bring their children into his presence.

Setting Spiritual Priorities

It's been said that time is our most valuable commodity. Life is busy, and many families today suffer from over-scheduling. Our days are packed with our normal, routine activities accented by special events, errands, sports, hobbies, and many other things—all of which combine to clutter our lives. A real danger for us parents is that we attempt to accomplish too many things in too little time. The end result is that we do not make the spiritual growth of our children a priority. Busyness keeps some parents from bringing their children to Jesus.

Chances are that many of the parents who read this book will be from a two-income family where both parents are employed outside the home. It is also very likely that at least one spouse in the family works in excess of forty hours per week. In addition to work, there are social events, sporting events, and spiritual events. Parents today have huge time demands placed on them, and many struggle when it comes to guarding valuable family time.

Fortunately, parents can clear up much of their scheduling dilemmas by following a few principles when it comes to how they spend their time.

First, parents need to prioritize. Moms and dads wear many different hats; we are called upon to be and do many things. Even though most, if not all, of these things are good, we must determine what is *best* and invest in those things first. For our consideration, let's look at a few of the roles parents must play. If we are married, we have the job of being a spouse. Parents must be providers. We have to be healers. We are friends and we are educators. Life can be a complicated maze of personal, parental, and vocational tasks. Decide what is important and what has value. You can better organize your life if you rank the importance of the many things you are called upon to do and give the most attention to the tasks with the most value.

The older I get, the better I am at saying no. I have learned (the hard way) that I *can* say no when it comes to acquiring new time commitments. Here is a truth that will set you free: If you do not set the limits of your own schedule, other people will. I encourage you to set the limits of your schedule and your children's schedule and then stick to those limits. One area in which our family has set limits is in the area of sports. Our kids are allowed to play only one sport at a time. This rule will sound reasonable to some people and unreasonable to others. My wife, Keli, and I have faced a great deal of pressure to fudge on this rule. The lion's share of pressure has not come from our children, but from our peers! Fathers and mothers should be the ones to set the limits on the combined schedule of their family.

A final word of wisdom is to set up a firewall between work and family. I confess a struggle in this area. When moms and dads leave work and come home, that is exactly what they should do—leave work! Computers should be put away and cell phones turned off. Certainly, as Christians we serve God by being the best employees we can possibly be. We strive to honor God with our work ethic, but our job is not our first responsibility. Our family comes before our vocation.

Parents on a Mission

Busyness is not a new problem for families. It was a problem two thousand years ago as well. The disciples knew that Jesus was busy preaching and teaching. They understood that he barely had a moment of time for himself. Jesus' disciples knew he had to sneak away just to have time to rest. Wanting to protect Jesus from what they thought were unimportant distractions, they told the parents not to bother him with the children (Luke 18:15). But what the disciples did not understand was how deeply

Jesus cared for children. They were not an intrusion: for Jesus, the spiritual welfare of these children was his *mission*.

Parents today, like the parents in Luke chapter eighteen, should be on a mission to take their children into the presence of Jesus. Life should never get so busy that parents do not have time to make the spiritual growth of their children their priority. Does your family need to slow down and reorganize its priorities?

It is important to mention here that churches should seize the opportunity to assist moms and dads as they pass their spiritual beliefs on to their children. Many churches need to reconsider the importance of a strong ministry to children. Often, children's ministry consists of baby-sitting while Dad and Mom are being fed spiritually. In fact, if the disciples were anything like the church today, they were probably trying to figure out a way to hire someone to watch the children while the parents went on retreat with Jesus! But the fact is, children are receptive to the gospel; they are hungry to learn about God's plan for their lives.

When Jesus heard what the disciples were saying to the parents, he responded, "Let the little children come to me, and do not hinder them, for the kingdom of God belongs to such as these" (Luke 18:16). From Jesus' response to the disciples, parents can gather at least three profound truths about the heart of our Lord for children.

A Parent's Greatest Privilege.

A parent's greatest privilege and greatest responsibility is to bring their children to Jesus. I have often wondered what kinds of obstacles the parents in Luke chapter eighteen overcame in order to bring their children to Jesus. I am sure that their lives were busy. Those parents had to have a schedule that included their employment, personal duties, and, to a lesser extent, leisure and hobbies. They must have overcome many obstacles and constraints in order to bring their children to Jesus.

As Jesus traveled and ministered, the word about him spread throughout the land. Parents would have heard about Jesus from other people who had either heard about Jesus or met him themselves. Two thousand years ago there were no trains, planes, or automobiles for traveling distances like we have today. Some of the parents who brought their children to be blessed by Jesus probably traveled great distances on foot. We can be sure that the parents two thousand years ago went to great lengths and overcame great obstacles to bring their children to Jesus. What are you willing to do to see that your child has an opportunity to know who Jesus is and have a personal relationship with him? What changes in lifestyle are you willing to embrace so that you can introduce your child to Jesus?

The Bible commands us to bring up our children "in the discipline and instruction of the lord" (Ephesians 6:4). Parents are only given one job in the Scriptures. Parents are to raise up spiritual children, and they will be held accountable to God for the spiritual instruction of their children. I can think of no greater task or privilege—and we only get one chance to get it right.

I remember when my wife's father gave her to me, standing at the altar during our wedding. I was so nervous that my feet were literally wet with sweat. When I took Keli's hand and turned to face the pastor, I thought I would walk right out of my shoes! That was probably the first time in my life that I felt responsible for someone else. But that day was a walk in the park compared to the day we had our first child. When our daughter was born, I looked at her and knew for the first time in my life that someone was completely dependent on me. At that moment I was so proud and frightened! I knew that I was entirely responsible for the physical and spiritual welfare of another human soul. Dad and Mom, you are responsible to God to introduce your children to his son. Whether they commit their lives to him or not will be their own personal decision; but, make no mistake, *you* must teach them about spiritual matters.

Fathers and mothers should look for ways to impart spiritual truth to their children in every experience of life. Life is full of opportunities to learn about the love, mercy, grace, and forgiveness of God. One day, for example, I got a call to pick up my daughter from school. When I arrived at the office, I could see that one of her eyes was swollen shut. She had been playing on the playground when one of her classmates kicked her in the eye, and now she was so upset she could not continue in school that day. This was a traumatic incident for a first grader, and she was very upset with the child who had kicked her.

I took my daughter home and left her in the care of her mom. No one can console a child like her mother! Keli listened to our daughter express her feelings of hurt and anger. In that tender moment, my wife was able to take the ugly incident and turn into an opportunity to teach our daughter about forgiveness.

Whose Responsibility Is it Anyway?

In my ministry I encourage moms and dads to be the ones who bring their children to Jesus. As a pastor I love to see children in church. I love to talk to them in the hallways, visit their Sunday school classes, and occasionally have a meal with them at our Wednesday night fellowship meals. But God has not given me the ultimate responsibility for their spiritual welfare. I am pastor to the children, and as such will be held accountable to God for how I shepherd them; but God has given the responsibility for the spiritual growth of these children to their parents. God did not give those precious children to me. He gave them to the fathers and mothers in my congregation.

In the book of Deuteronomy, God instructs fathers and mothers to teach their children all that he had taught them: "Fix these words of mine in your hearts and minds; tie them as symbols on your hands and bind them on your foreheads. Teach them to your children, talking about them when you sit at home and when you walk along the road, when you lie down and when you get up" (Deuteronomy 11:18–19). The writer of Proverbs advises parents to "Train up a child in the way he should go: and when he is old, he will not depart from it" (Proverbs 22:6 KJV). There are many Scripture verses that illustrate the responsibility of parents to give their children spiritual instruction, but there are none that place that responsibility on the pastor. The closest the Bible comes to giving responsibility for the spiritual instruction of children is with regard to *his own children*: "An elder must be blameless, the husband of but one wife, a man whose children believe and are not open to the charge of being wild and disobedient" (Titus 1:6).

My role as a pastor according to Scripture is "to prepare God's people for works of service, so that the body of Christ may be built up" (Ephesians 4:12). This means my responsibility is to prepare parents to bring their children to Christ and to equip them to carry out their responsibility. The ultimate privilege and responsibility for raising up spiritual children belongs to parents. God's plan is for fathers and mothers to bring their children to Jesus.

As parents, we love our children, and we try to do the best things for them. We provide for them, spend time with them, and teach them about life. Parents do lots of good things for their children; but the best thing parents can do is to invest spiritually in their children. The spiritual development of our children matters more than any other form of development. We must put as much, or more, energy into our children's spiritual development as their physical and intellectual development. The lesson the disciples learned two thousand years ago bears repeating today: the Savior, whose love is perfect, loves our children even more than we do.

Forbid Not the Children.

A second truth to consider is that parents should never do anything to hinder a child who wants to know Jesus. In Luke chapter eighteen, the disciples should have been helping parents bring children to Jesus, but instead they were trying to keep them away from Jesus. I have encountered a handful of parents who have kept their children from following Jesus. Some parents intentionally keep their children from knowing about Jesus, and others keep their children from knowing Jesus by their unintentional actions and attitudes.

Once, in my ministry, I encountered a couple whose preteen child had made a faith commitment to Jesus in vacation Bible school at our church. The parents claimed to be Christians but attended church infrequently. They refused to let their daughter be baptized and join the church. Perhaps they thought their child was too young to make a decision that important. Maybe guilt about their own spiritual failures kept them from encouraging their daughter's spiritual growth. It's possible they thought that they would have to become spiritually committed if their children were. Whatever the reason behind the parents' motives, the end result was that the girl was not allowed to grow spiritually. That young girl, now an adult, is not active in any church. Instead of nurturing their daughter's newfound faith, they extinguished it. Their lack of involvement in her spiritual life led to her own spiritual indifference and apathy.

Some parents will stifle the spiritual interest of a child because they feel the child does not know enough or is not old enough. Other parents hinder spiritual growth in their children because they themselves do not have time for spiritual matters. I have seen parents tell children they cannot make a faith commitment because their behavior is not good enough. Most commonly, parents do not nurture the spiritual lives of their children because of their own spiritual apathy. It is less trouble to sleep in on Sunday morning than it is to take the children to church.

Every community has parents who intentionally or unintentionally hinder the spiritual growth of their children. But children are precious to our Lord and they have a need to know him! Parents need to discover the truth that their spiritual responsibility before God is to bring their children to Jesus. Children can know Jesus and—make no mistake—our Lord desires the attention, affection, and worship of children.

Matthew 18:6 gives insight into the heart of Jesus for children: "But if anyone causes one of these little ones who believe in me to sin, it would be better for him to have a large millstone hung around his neck and to be drowned in the depths of the sea." It is safe to say that Jesus does not want parents, disciples, or anyone else to hinder the spiritual growth of children. One day parents, pastors, coaches, neighbors, relatives, and friends will answer to God for discouraging instead of encouraging the spiritual growth of children.

The Faith of a Child.

Third, Luke 18:17 teaches that there is only one way to be saved: "I tell you the truth, anyone who will not receive the kingdom of God like a little child will never enter it." People enter a relationship with God when they have the faith of a child. Adults and children enter heaven in the same way. Salvation is not about what we know or do. It comes from a childlike faith in Christ and what he has done on our behalf on the cross. It has been said that there are only two kinds of people who go to heaven. First, there are little children and second, there are those who enter like little children. To be spiritually right with God, one must come to his son, Jesus, with the simplicity, openness, and total dependence of a child.

Children Belong to God

The Bible teaches in Psalm 139:13–14 that God has created each child, and in that sense they already belong to him: "For you created my inmost being; you knit me together in my mother's womb. I praise you because I am fearfully and wonderfully made; your works are wonderful, I know that full well." It is God's desire for every child to be returned to him. When parents bring their children to Jesus, they are ultimately bringing them to the very one who has created them.

In some churches, parents will formalize a commitment to bring their children to Jesus in a baby dedication service. But if parents are to fulfill their spiritual obligation to their heavenly Father, they will bring their children to their creator every day. Spiritual instruction should take place not just on Sunday, but every day.

Jesus' heart beats for children. Churches and parents have the privilege of mirroring the heart of Jesus for children. Parents must be as available and open to children as our Lord was. If parents are to fulfill their spiritual obligation to their heavenly Father, they will bring their children to Jesus.

Chapter Two

Lessons from Godly Relationships

Husbands, love your wives, just as Christ loved the church and gave himself up for her to make her holy, cleansing her by the washing with water through the word, and to present her to himself as a radiant church, without stain or wrinkle or any other blemish, but holy and blameless. In this same way, husbands ought to love their wives as their own bodies. He who loves his wife loves himself. (Ephesians 5:25–28)

Be perfect, therefore, as your heavenly Father is perfect. (Matthew 5:48)

Family Relationships Reflect God

In my ministry I encounter every kind of family relationship: those which are open and thriving, those which are closed and damaged by adversity, and those which swing either direction according to what life is dealing out at the moment. Over the course of years, I have known quite a few really terrific families; but I can honestly say that I have never seen the *perfect* family or *perfect* marriage. If your family is like mine, you have moments when your family looks like the best in the world and other times when you are glad no one is looking.

Yet it is in the dynamics of our family relationships that children learn about God. They will associate good or bad feelings when they think about God as our Father in heaven depending upon whether or not they have experienced satisfying family relationships. If, for example, a dad effectively fulfills his duty as a Christian father, his children will find it easy to see God as a Good Father. The relationships our children encounter in life will become a filter through which they view the world and understand spiritual concepts. By reflecting the nature and character of God in our families, we can create an environment that nurtures spiritual growth and helps children embrace the gospel. What, then, *is* the character of God toward us, his children?

The Perfect Parent

The Bible tells us that God is the perfect parent (Matthew 5:48). God's Word also teaches: "Yet to all who received him, to those who believed in his name, he gave the right to become children of God" (John 1:12).

We can be sure that, as his children, God lavishes his love on us (1 John 3:1). We are as dependent upon the loving care of God as our children are on our love and care. Since the relationship of parent and child is a metaphor for the relationship between God and his children, how we relate as parents to our children will one day become a pattern for how they understand the nature and character of God. God is our heavenly parent, and he is perfect in every way. While we cannot achieve the perfection of our heavenly Father, we can demonstrate the same characteristics he displays towards his children.

God Like a Father

As we read the Bible, we discover the metaphor of God as a father to his spiritual children. That relationship started in the Garden of Eden with the first set of human parents, Adam and Eve. In the Sermon on the Mount, Jesus commands us to "Be perfect, therefore, as your heavenly *Father* is perfect" (Matthew 5:48, emphasis added). Jesus also began the model prayer with the words: "Our *Father* in heaven . . ." (Matthew 6:9, emphasis added). The fatherhood of God is an image that permeates both the Old and New Testaments.

The word *father* brings out a variety of feelings and emotions for everyone who hears it. For some the word *father* invokes warm emotions. I am thankful for all of the dads out there who model godliness to their children.

People who have had a loving relationship with their father can easily see the image of God as a caring Father. It is my prayer that in my own life I do not tarnish the image of God the Father by my behavior as a dad.

Tragically, not all of us have those same happy memories and not all have grown up with the influence of a godly father. While there are many good fathers, there are plenty of fathers who do not serve as good role models. Some fathers are distant and uncaring; others are abusive and unfaithful. So many children cannot conceive of a perfect, loving heavenly Father because that hasn't been part of their experience on earth. If you are a dad reading this book let me encourage you to look to the example set by our heavenly Father as a pattern for parenting your own children. There is a parallel between our relationship as being children of God and being fathers of our children. When we are good children in our relationship with our heavenly Father, we will be good parents to the children God has entrusted to us.

God Like a Mother

The Bible compares some of God's most tender behaviors toward us to the compassion, comfort, and love of a mother. Likewise, moms can find the perfect pattern for their maternal relationships by looking to our Creator for their example. God's Word states, "Can a mother forget the baby at her breast and have no compassion on

Notes

1 "Conversion and Witnessing Among Southern Baptist,"
Research services of the North American Mission Board of
the Southern Baptist Convention, http://www.namb.net/root/
resources/stats/Baptism%20Indicators%202000.pdf

2 Erin Anderson, "The Key to TV is Limiting and Controlling
What Kids Watch," *Lincoln Journal Star* (May 9, 2004),
http://www.journalstar.com/articles/2004/04/16/hubbub/
10048235.txt.

3 "Children: How They Grow, Elementary School Children
Ages 6 to 8," Karen B. DeBord, www.classbrain.com/artread/
publish/article_36.shtml.

4 http://childparenting.about.com/childdevelopment/a/
eightyearold3.

5 As a Baptist pastor I believe that baptism is not essential
to salvation but is essential for obedience to the commands
of Christ and the fulfilling of the great commission found
in chapter twenty-eight of the Gospel of Matthew. In the
New Testament we first see baptism being performed by
John the Baptist when he ushered in the ministry of Jesus by
baptizing people who repented of their sins (Matthew 3:6;
Mark 1:4). People came to John to be baptized and to mark a
new beginning in their lives as they confessed their sins and
renewed their spiritual commitment to God. For Jesus, the
practice of baptism was an event that marked a change in a
person's life so significant that he himself was baptized by

and the baby went to his lawyer's office to complete the paperwork. The lawyer took the child's original birth certificate and set it on fire. He then took a brand new birth certificate bearing the child's new name and gave it to the parents. It is the same when we come to God through Christ—we have a new parent and a new name. The old has passed away and we have been made new creations in Christ (2 Corinthians 5:17).

Bringing Family Relationships into Harmony with God's Perfect Example

God is the perfect parent and, as such, he demonstrates to us in perfection everything that is right and good about the relationship between parent and child. But our lives too provide a dictionary from which our children will understand the words that describe the nature of God. As parents, we can provide good definitions for our children by living out the attributes of God toward them. Healthy, loving family relationships will create an environment that nurtures spiritual growth and helps children embrace the gospel. For that reason, let's take a look at the pattern of God's ideal relationships.

God's Ideal for Marriage

Scripture sets forth a pattern and an ideal of how the marriage relationship should be. We see that pattern throughout the Bible, but particularly in Ephesians, chapter five, where marriage is used as a metaphor to describe Christ's relationship to his church. A loving marriage is a picture of a loving Lord who gave himself freely for us. When a mother and father love each other as Jesus loved the church and are willing to give themselves fully for each other, they create a secure environment for the physical, emotional, intellectual, and spiritual growth of a child.

I recently heard the story of a husband who came home from work, took a pan of water, and washed his wife's feet. He was following the example of Jesus found in John, chapter thirteen. Jesus washed the feet of his disciples, then said, "Now that I, your Lord and Teacher, have washed your feet, you also should wash one another's feet."

This loving husband was communicating to his wife that he valued her above himself and loved her with a servant-love. He was demonstrating to his wife how much she meant to him. Parents can teach a deep spiritual lesson to their children by loving and serving each another.

The bottom line is that God wants us to bring the *reality* of our marriage closer to the *ideal* of marriage. He wants us to enjoy loving relationships that mirror the relationship Christ has with the church. He wants parents to have the kind of self-sacrificing love for each other illustrated in Ephesians 5 because it demonstrates the gospel in action to our children and creates a family environment that is ideal for the spiritual training of children.

Practice Forgiveness

When two people share their lives (time, home, family, and goals) with each other, invariably the need for forgiveness will arise. It has been said that we are *least like Christ* when we refuse to forgive and *most like Christ* when we do forgive. If forgiveness is needed for our lives in this world, how much more is it needed in our marriages? In the Sermon on the Mount, Jesus taught his followers to ask God for forgiveness as they forgive others: "Keep us forgiven with you and forgiving others" (Matthew 6:12 THE MESSAGE). Jesus also taught that our forgiveness by God is contingent upon our forgiving others: "Do not judge, and you will not be judged. Do not condemn, and you will not be condemned. Forgive, and you will be forgiven" (Luke 6:37).

Forgiveness is needed in every marriage, but more in some than others. Many times couples bicker over trivial things, but sometimes the issues that cause conflict are not so trivial, and the task of forgiving is not so easy. Nevertheless, Scripture warns about the result of unforgiveness: "If you keep on biting and devouring each other, watch out or you will be destroyed by each other" (Galatians 5:15).

The burden of unforgiveness and the emotional chaos it causes can be devastating. It can destroy a marriage and stunt the spiritual growth of children.

In some families, parents expect their children to forgive each other but do not demonstrate the same standard they ask of their children. In others, an angry spouse will forgive, but only after making the mate pay dearly for his or her offense. Instead of continuing the fight and holding on to hurt and grudges, moms and dads should strive to follow the instructions of Scripture to forgive, comfort, and reaffirm their love for each other (2 Corinthians 2:7–8).

Whether we give it or not, forgiveness has great power to heal and instruct. When we forgive, we teach our children how to give and receive forgiveness. When we refuse to forgive, we teach our children to live in hurt and to be revengeful. Couples can teach their children to live in the power of a new future when they practice forgiveness. The need for forgiveness is an essential part of the Gospel. We all need forgiveness because we have all committed sin against God (Romans 3:23). By practicing forgiveness in our homes, we can demonstrate to our children how to live free from guilt. We can show them the importance of asking for and receiving forgiveness.

Family First

The family was God's first institution. Even before God gave us the church, he gave us the family as a sanctuary for spiritual instruction. Parents who love and serve one another in front of their children teach them valuable lessons about giving, sacrifice, compromise, love, affection, and ultimately about a Savior who gave his life for them.

Jesus' love for the church is the model the Bible gives for the relationship between husband and wife. He displayed his love for the church for the world to see as he died on the cross. Husbands and wives should also display their love and commitment to one another in an open fashion. I believe children are strengthened when they see their parents openly displaying appropriate affection for each other in the home, and they thrive in the security of seeing their parents in a love relationship. Perhaps the greatest spiritual instruction of all is a love relationship between a father and mother who are husband and wife first.

When Life Takes a Detour

Last week I was out running some errands and needed to go to Wal-Mart. As I got close to the intersection for my turn, I noticed more road construction than was normal for the superstore. As I approached, things quickly became a mess. There were dump trucks, bulldozers, guys wearing hard hats and orange vests, and more orange cones and barrels than I had ever before seen in one place. There were signs up and down the street with arrows announcing a detour, so in the midst of the construction, barrels, orange cones, workers, equipment, and traffic I took a detour. My easy drive to the store did not turn out as I planned. In fact, I ended up somewhere I had never been, and I wasn't sure how to get back to where I needed to be. Eventually, I did manage to finish my errands, but not without considerable effort to get back on the right road.

At times life is like that detour—it just doesn't work out the way we planned. Sometimes we ourselves make poor choices that affect ourselves and our families, and sometimes other people make harmful decisions that affect our lives in profound ways. God's word has some instruction for us which will help us maintain a home environment that fosters spiritual development no matter how many twists, turns, and detours we have taken on life's road.

Few people begin their adult life with plans to be divorced or abandoned, or to raise their children without the aid of a loving spouse. Most of us dream about having the perfect home with the perfect spouse and the perfect job only to wake up one day to find things aren't really so perfect. There are few guarantees in life, and detours are plentiful. The reality of this statement raises a serious question: What do you do when you find that you are a twenty-eight-year-old single parent of two who wants her children to know God in a real and personal way? When life takes a detour, how do you create a home environment favorable to your children's spiritual growth?

If life for you has taken a detour and you find yourself alone in the task of passing on your spiritual beliefs to your children, no matter what the circumstances are you can find comfort in the fact that God has called you to be a parent and has himself provided both the tools and the example for you to do this. Whether you are single, single again, have a blended family, or are married to someone who does not share your beliefs, *you* are called by God to nurture your child spiritually. God does not dismiss us from that sweet responsibility. The writer of Proverbs admonishes all parents to "train a child in the way he should go, and when he is old he will not turn from it" (Proverbs 22:6). This instruction applies whether we come from a traditional or non-traditional family.

I love to play golf. I am not a good golfer, but I do enjoy the game. In general, golf is not a very forgiving sport. There are many hazards and rules with penalties to match when those rules are broken. But there is one thing I really appreciate about the game of golf. I love the *mulligan rule*. If you hit a bad shot off the tee, you can have a mulligan—another chance to hit the ball where it belongs. The beautiful thing about a mulligan is that we can admit our imperfection, and then we get another chance! A mulligan is grace at work on the golf course. Parents all need an extra measure of grace, whether they are single or have a mate to share the responsibilities. The good news is that our heavenly Father is a forgiving God who abounds in grace (1 John 1:9).

In the Old Testament when God's chosen people had taken a detour, the prophet Jeremiah told them to, "Stand at the crossroads and look; ask for the ancient paths, ask where the good way is, and walk in it, and you will find rest for your souls" (Jeremiah 6:16). What God was telling the people of Israel through the prophet holds true for us today. Jeremiah told the people to get back to being who God intended them to be. Redirecting life after a detour is not easy, but God will not leave you alone (see Deuteronomy 31:1–6). When life takes a detour we must go back to the path that God has laid out for us to travel. Don't give in, and don't quit. Do your best to create an environment that nurtures spiritual growth, and be the parent God wants you to be, modeling yourself after his own perfect pattern of parenthood.

Characteristics of Parent–Child Relationship

Scripture gives parents plenty of guidance on how to parent our children to bring about spiritual growth.

The Father's Unconditional Love

As parents, our love for our children should be unconditional. We should be driven to love our children whether they succeed or fail. They deserve our love whether they are introverted or extroverted, popular or unpopular, obedient or rebellious. Regardless of the direction our children choose to take in life, we must love them. As a pastor I have, on numerous occasions, met parents whose children have made a mess of their lives and have hurt everyone around them—but the parents love them any way. What a blessing those parents are! I believe that the parent who displays unconditional love for his or her child displays the kind of love God has for us. Choices both bad and good in life may affect our relationships with our children, but those choices can never be allowed to sever the relationships we have with our children. We should strive to help them understand that we will never disown them. If the love we have for our children is to reflect the love our heavenly Father has for us, it will never be contingent upon behavior or performance.

One of the greatest Scriptures on the unconditional love of God is Romans 5:8 which says, "But God demonstrates his own love for us in this: While we were still sinners, Christ died for us." This verse lets us know that God loved us even when we weren't lovable. He loves us with a love that is not conditional upon our good behavior or lost because of our bad behavior. As a parent, I try to instill in my children the truth that I love them even when they misbehave and come under discipline. I try never to discipline my children without telling them that I love them. Children can learn about the love of God when we love them without condition just as God first loved us.

A Patient Father

The story of the prodigal son found in Luke, chapter fifteen, provides one of the most enduring images of God as a patient father in all of Scripture. In this parable, Jesus told the story of a man who had two sons. One son was submissive and obedient, but the younger son was wayward and headstrong. The father graciously gave to the young son his inheritance, and the boy took off to enjoy life. I believe the father knew the son well enough to know that he was going to waste both his life and his money—which he did as fast as was humanly possible. The picture Jesus painted of this young man was that of a rebellious young man whose behaviour must have hurt his family deeply. The father in the parable is a picture of the heavenly Father, and the son represents all who have left the way and will of the father to live as they see fit.

God knows us and he knows our hearts just as the father in this parable knew his son. The father patiently waited and watched for his son to come home. When he did return, the father rejoiced. The father had every right to reject the son when he returned home, but he did not. The father forgave and restored the son to his position within the family.

Aren't you glad our God is a patient God? Can you think of some times when God must have had to wait for you to come to your senses and return to him? Parents who portray the patient love of the Father in heaven are parents who are willing to wait patiently for a rebellious child to come home. If God is anything toward his children, he is patient.

Our God is the God of second chances. The prodigal son took what he thought he had a right to and went out in the world to make his own way. He thought he was advancing his life, but what he was really doing was losing ground. Perhaps as a teenager you were prodigal and lost ground spiritually, or maybe you have a child who is. We can learn a valuable lesson about regaining lost ground from this parable.

Parents must practice forgiveness. The father of the prodigal son was taken for granted and disrespected. The son was arrogant, assuming, and selfish. To make matters worse, the son brought shame on the family name while he was living his own way. Clearly, the father had been wronged. Yet, we can see by his actions toward the son that he had forgiven him even before the son repented of his sins and returned home. Jesus said, "But while he was still a long way off, his father saw him and was filled with compassion for him; he ran to his son, threw his arms around him and kissed him" (Luke 15:20). The family was restored and the son was in a position to regain lost ground because of the forgiveness of the father.

We can help our children regain lost ground by restoring their dignity. Rebellion will ultimately lead to shame and embarrassment. The son in the story was ready to go back to the father and be as one of his servants (Luke 15:18–19). The son knew he had offended his father and did not deserve to be reinstated to his former place of honor. However, the response of the father was the key to his restoration: "The father said to his servants, 'Quick! Bring the best robe and put it on him. Put a ring on his finger and sandals on his feet. Bring the fattened calf and kill it. Let's have a feast and celebrate. For this son of mine was dead and is alive again; he was lost and is found.' So they began to celebrate" (Luke 15:22–24). When our children fail (and they will), we must let them know that we love and accept them.

A Disciplining Father

Our God is a God of love and of patience, but he is also a God of discipline. The discipline of God began in the Garden of Eden with Adam and Eve, continues throughout Scripture, and ends in the last chapter of the Bible with a warning that anyone who adds to or takes away from the book of Revelation will come under the discipline of God. Like it or not, we are like God when we discipline our children. I have yet to meet a loving parent who did not believe in discipline. I would go so far as to say that a parent who will not discipline his or her child is selfish and does not have the best interest of that child at heart. For our children to understand God, they need to have an understanding of discipline.

Discipline is so much a part of who we are as believers that there is a warning in Hebrews chapter twelve for those who do not come under the discipline of God. The writer of Hebrews warns that those who do not come under the discipline of God are illegitimate children (Hebrews 12:8). He also writes that discipline is for our good and will produce a "harvest of righteousness" in our lives (Hebrews 12:11). Proper discipline prepares children to understand this spiritual concept.

I do not like to come under discipline myself, nor do I enjoy bringing discipline on my children, but I understand we all need to be corrected from time to time. While I was in seminary, a wise man told me that discipline does no good unless we understand the reason why we are being disciplined in the first place. He told me that I should always tell my children before and after I disciplined them why it was that they were being disciplined. If you read the Bible through from Genesis to Revelation, you will find that God never administered punishment without telling his children why he was disciplining them.

In short, discipline teaches our children about consequences. When God disciplines us we learn that there are consequences for trying to go through life doing things our way. When we discipline our children, we help them to understand the truth that there are consequences when we reject God's way.

A Providing Father

A final picture of God as parent in Scripture is that of a benevolent and giving provider. In the Sermon on the Mount, Jesus compares the desire of earthly fathers to give good gifts with the desire of our heavenly Father. He said, "If you, then, though you are evil, know how to give good gifts to your children, how much more will your Father in heaven give good gifts to those who ask him" (Matthew 7:11). As good parents we want to give our children the very best of everything. But Jesus said that our heavenly Father is even better at giving good gifts to his children!

God's love can be characterized as being unconditional and so can his giving. Our God is so good that he gives whether we are appreciative or not. God gives and blesses people every day whether or not they recognize where the gifts of life come from. God perfects the art of parenthood by blessing the grateful and the ungrateful alike: "He causes his sun to rise on the evil and the good, and sends rain on the righteous and the unrighteous" (Matthew 5:45). God sets the example for all parents by giving even when his children are ungrateful. As parents we should give to our children, not to manipulate their behavior but rather to mimic the unconditional nature of the giving of God.

Chances are your children do not realize all of the things you as a parent do for them. I would venture to say that there have been some great things you have done for your children which went unappreciated. Parents who give to their children as God gives do not provide for their children because they deserve it or because they owe it to them. Parents take care of the needs of their children because they love them and want the best for them. As parents we reflect the nature of God to our children when we provide generously for our children.

Christian parents want to provide for their children physically, emotionally, and intellectually like all other parents. But even more important, Christian parents want their children to know who God is and what God wants for them in their lives. Throughout Scripture, the way God relates to us, his children, is an example to us of how God would have us to relate to our children. When Christian parents reflect the parental nature of God to their children, we enable them to see God as a loving, compassionate, disciplining, caring, and providing Father.

Chapter Three

How to Build an Environment for Evangelism in the Home

Fix these words of mine in your hearts and minds; tie them as symbols on your hands and bind them on your foreheads. Teach them to your children, talking about them when you sit at home and when you walk along the road, when you lie down and when you get up. Write them on the doorframes of your houses and on your gates, so that your days and the days of your children may be many in the land that the LORD swore to give your forefathers, as many as the days that the heavens are above the earth. (Deuteronomy 11:18–21)

Where to Start?

I had the privilege of being present at the births of all three of my children. After the doctors and nurses had weighed and taken the measurements of our children, we were encouraged to hold those precious babies. The medical professionals understood that the bonding process between parent and baby needed to happen right away. I am convinced that this is true spiritually as well. Parents can and should facilitate the bonding of child and Creator from his or her first days.

Laying a foundation for spiritual beliefs in the heart of a child begins in the nursery. Mothers and fathers can impart spiritual truth to their children while they are still infants. My wife and I began laying the spiritual foundations for our children even before they could walk or talk, and now their spiritual lives are as much a part of who they are as their physical beings.

Children need to grow spiritually as much as they do physically. In the book of Proverbs the Bible admonishes parents to, "Train a child in the way he should go, and when he is old he will not turn from it" (Proverbs 22:6). This biblical principle underscores the parent's role as a spiritual teacher and not just a physical provider in the lives of his children. In the early days of childhood, physical, intellectual, social, and emotional growth occurs at a rapid pace. The same should be true of their spiritual growth. Moms and dads need to realize the spiritual growth potential of their little children. A successful father of three once told me that a parent can impart a spiritual worldview into the lives of his or her children by giving them spiritual instruction for the first five years of their lives. He and his wife had paid close attention to the spiritual development of their children early in their children's lives. Their investment has paid off in a big way. Their kids are all married with their own families, and all three are still deeply committed to following God with their lives. Since we all acknowledge our desire to see our children become lifelong disciples of Christ, let's look at some things parents can do to plant spiritual truth in the lives of their children.

The Power of Music

Music is a wonderful way for parents to begin to communicate the love of God to their children. From the day our children were born, Keli and I have sung songs like "God is so Good," "Jesus Loves Me," and "Jesus Loves the Little Children." When we as parents sing songs of faith to our children, we teach them to associate the name of our Lord with love and security. Music may be the single most effective way to teach spiritual truth to our children. Children's songs have the power to stay with us for a lifetime. Did you learn any of the songs previously mentioned as a child? If you did, I'm sure you still remember them!

Now that my children are older they like to sing worship songs like "Shout to the Lord" or "I Could Sing of Your Love Forever." When Keli and I became parents, we sang *to* our children about God's love; now we sing *with* our children about his love. We are passing our faith on to our children through music. Music is a fun and interactive way for parents to nurture the spiritual growth of their children.

My children were given a book of Bible songs by some of our church members a couple of years ago. This book contains some wonderful hymns like "What a Friend We Have in Jesus," "All Things Bright and Beautiful," and "In the Garden." Teaching our children hymns has great value. They are rich in doctrine, inspiration, and encouragement. When we teach our children those great songs of the faith, we are teaching them more than a song. We are teaching them spiritual truths that will stick with them for the rest of their lives. Singing with your children is a powerful way to include biblical instruction with play time.

Baby Talk

Do not underestimate the importance of speaking spiritual truths to babies. Parents can have a significant spiritual impact on infant children and toddlers by telling them about God's love. Babies respond to the facial expressions and the tone of voice of the person holding them. Parents can begin to build a spiritual foundation within their infant by telling them about God's love while they hold them, rock them, or feed them.

Babies learn the words *Mommy* and *Daddy* very early in life. When they hear the sound of their parents' names, they light up. Babies can learn to associate those same feelings of delight with the name of God by the way their parents talk to them while they hold them. Parents can impart truth to a baby while lovingly telling them how much love God feels for them. Parents can assure their baby that they are special to God and that he has created them. It is never too early to begin to reinforce basic spiritual truths to your child. If parents wait until their child can talk before they tell that child about the love of God, they have missed many precious months and valuable opportunities to nurture the spiritual development of their children.

Bible Stories

Young children learn spiritual truths as their parents read them Bible stories written on a level appropriate for their age and understanding. Follow these times with questions and answers or a craft related to the story just read to cement the spiritual truths introduced. There are many great products available at Christian bookstores. You will find a list of great read-along books in the appendix of this book. My children love coloring books. There are many coloring books on the market that portray a favorite Bible story or have a biblical theme. Parents can relate the Bible story while the child colors the picture. Over the years we have proudly displayed many works of biblical art made by little hands.

At some point in their development, your children will be able to recount Bible stories to you. Children love to tell stories, and telling stories is a great way to reinforce memory. In our home we have regular story-telling sessions. Usually our story times begin with me starting the story and my children finishing it. Sometimes they get stumped and cannot remember the story. When this happens I will prompt them with the answer, or sometimes I simply ask them, "What happened next?" I love story time with my kids and the truth is that I probably get as much out of it as they do.

Arts and Crafts

Allowing children to create a project that is tied to a spiritual truth can have a lasting spiritual impact. One Sunday my daughter's Sunday school class did an art project that made quite an impression on us parents—and on our daughter as well. The teacher gave every child a dish of plaster and encouraged each one to press his or her hand into the mold leaving an imprint in the plaster. On each plaster mold they wrote Psalm 139:14: "I praise you because I am fearfully and wonderfully made; your works are wonderful, I know that full well." The lesson for the day was that God is the Creator; he has made every child special, and he loves them all. Involving the plaster craft in the lesson did not make it any more true; but it certainly made it more memorable.

Children love to color and design. They work puzzles and do crafts almost every day. Why not take the opportunities our children give us to teach a spiritual lesson? Parents can use play dough to teach a lesson about almost any Bible theme. Legos and building blocks can be used to recount the story of Joshua and the Battle of Jericho. Moms baking bread with their children can teach a lesson about Jesus being the Bread of Life. A visit to the zoo can become a story about Noah's ark. Dads can use a small garden or even a potted plant to teach children that God makes things grow. Parents can use even a simple task like washing dirty hands to teach about forgiveness. There are teachable moments all around us—all we have to do is watch for the opportunities. The more creativity moms and dads use, the more memorable and interesting the spiritual truth will be to their children. Our God is a God of creativity. All around us we can see his handiwork. He has designed us to be creative as well.

Prayer Time

Prayer is one of the best ways to create an environment for evangelism in the home. Children learn quickly through prayer that God is our provider. Prayer teaches children to look to God for the needs of life. Parents should pray with and for their children.

Prayer has become a natural part of our children's lives. Keli and I have taught children to pray at mealtime, bedtime, and other special times. They love to pray, and often all three will take turns praying before a meal. We have encouraged our children to pray about everything. They are now at the point in their faith where they bring prayer requests to us. We pray together for teachers and sick friends and other things that concern them.

Truth You Can See

Christian videos are wonderful tools parents can use to teach spiritual truth to children. Children today watch far too much television. According to Time Warner Cable, children under the age of six watch up to two hours of television per day, and children between the ages of six and seventeen watch three hours or more per day—not counting the three or more hours they spend on the computer or playing video games.[2] Unfortunately, many of the cartoon characters on the cartoon networks are not good role models for our children. Cartoon characters often teach lessons based upon someone else's values. They often use language we as parents would not allow from our children, commit random acts of violence without any thought to consequences, and display poor behavior choices when things do not go the way they would like them to go. I am convinced that parents need to limit, as much as possible, the amount of secular cartoons children watch and maximize their own personal involvement in the growth of their children.

While many television programs and video games do not offer positive role models for our children, plenty of wholesome alternatives are available. One of the most popular resources available today is the *Veggie Tales* series. These cartoon videos teach Bible stories and Christian values on a child's level. There are many other children's videos for parents to choose from. I have listed some good children's video series in Appendix C of this book.

Parents can and should create an environment for evangelism in the home. Parents who begin to build a spiritual foundation in the home while children are small are often rewarded. More often than not, their children will embrace the gospel message at an early age. It is never too early to begin the process of helping children develop spiritual beliefs.

Chapter Four
Partnering with the Church

And let us consider how we may spur one another on toward love and good deeds. Let us not give up meeting together, as some are in the habit of doing, but let us encourage one another—and all the more as you see the Day approaching. (Hebrews 10:24–25)

We Need Each Other

Evangelizing our children starts in the home and it starts early. Parents should be proactive about the evangelism of their children. Parents are not left without help and resources; the church can play a significant role in the evangelism of children and can *partner* with them to bring their children to Jesus. I am thankful for the ways that our church has partnered with us as a family in the spiritual development of our children

Ever since God first called his chosen people out of Egypt, he has assembled groups of his followers (the Church) for the purpose of the spiritual instruction of families. In the book of Deuteronomy, we see how God uses his church in the disciple-making process with children. God instructs Moses to "assemble the people before me to hear my words so that they may learn to revere me as long as they live in the land and may teach them to their children" (Deuteronomy 4:10). In another passage in Deuteronomy, Moses directs parents to teach their children what had been taught when they were assembled together (Deuteronomy 11:18–20). Children can learn from the direct teaching of Christians besides their parents, and they can also learn about what it means to be a Christian by watching how a church worships God as a community of faith.

In the New Testament, the writer of Hebrews instructs us on the importance of the church in our own spiritual development: "And let us consider how we may spur one another on toward love and good deeds. Let us not give up meeting together, as some are in the habit of doing, but let us encourage one another—and all the more as you see the Day approaching" (Hebrews 10:24–25). The local church can be a great encouragement and resource for parents who are concerned about passing on their spiritual legacy to their children.

Some parents believe they can or should depend wholly on the church to bring their child to Christ. We have already seen in chapter one of this book that it is the *parents* who are charged with the responsibility of bringing their children to the Lord. But the church *can* help. Within the church the efforts of mothers and fathers to disciple their children can be multiplied, and a child's spiritual maturity will increase with the encouragement, nurturing, and support of a community of faith.

Christians Should Worship Together

God has designed us to need each other. In the Christian life, our faith must be our own, but it is never to be lived out alone. In the tenth chapter of Hebrews, God's Word encourages Christians to be a part of a local group that gathers together regularly for worship. Scripture admonishes us to "see how inventive we can be in encouraging love and helping out" (Hebrews 10:24 THE MESSAGE). At church, our fellow Christians have loved, taught, and encouraged my family physically, emotionally, and spiritually.

A local church should be a *community* of believers who want to see children come to know Jesus as their Savior and want to help parents impart spiritual truth into the lives of their children. If you do not have a church home at this time, I would like to encourage you to find one. A church should be a place of love and acceptance where a child is recognized as a special gift from God. Things such as worship style, friendship, location, and programs offered can help parents identify a church that will assist in their children's spiritual training. However, the most important issue to resolve when looking for a church is that of doctrinal integrity. Does the church teach that the Bible is God's Word? Once you have found a Bible-teaching church, you will find that there are many ways the church can nurture the spiritual development of your children.

There is, for example, a group of senior adults at the church where I am pastor who got together one day and decided that they would become surrogate grandparents for the children in the congregation. They sat with the children in church, remembered birthdays, helped celebrate special occasions, and offered spiritual encouragement. My daughter had one special "grandfather" who would take her to eat breakfast at a local restaurant on from time to time. My children have been blessed by those special relationships and over the years have enjoyed many sets of grandparents.

Church Provides Encouragement for Parents

The church can be a support group for parents who want to lead their children to Jesus. Because I am a minister, we have never had the luxury of living close to our extended families. In the job market today, it is not uncommon for young adults to go off to college and then settle in another town or even another state from their parents. I realize that my family is not the only family that does not live near their parents. But over the years there have been many times when we have wished for the input and wisdom of our families during those challenging parenting times that our children provide for us. Our church has provided the encouragement that we would have gotten from our parents. They have been with us through both good and bad times.

Many churches today recognize that young families need the encouragement and godly support found in a Christian social environment. For this reason, many churches offer clubs, small groups, classes, and ministries designed to encourage and equip parents. My wife and I enjoy attending a Sunday school class for young couples at our church. The class is special to us because we are all close to the same age and are going through similar life experiences. Most of us are dealing with issues of budgeting our money, parenting, relationships, and time. Most importantly we are all trying to honor God with our lives. Sunday school classes for parents, whether single or married, are helpful because they enable people with the same struggles, needs, and goals to edify each other spiritually. It can be extremely encouraging to learn that other parents are going through the same struggles with kids that you and your spouse are going through.

The Church Works Like Math

That same class is a blessing to us as a family because the people in it provide the encouragement and companionship my wife and I need as we go through both the happy and the challenging times of raising children. When we share a sorrow with our class, the sorrow is *divided*. Not long ago a young couple in our church lost a baby—a devastating experience for them. God used the couples in the church to help carry the load of sorrow they felt. The church cried with this couple, counseled with them, prayed for them, and ministered to their physical needs. If you were to ask them today how they made it through that dark time in their lives, I am sure that they would tell you that they could not have made it without that fellowship of believers.

When my wife and I share a joy with our friends in the small group, it is *multiplied*. Some of the greatest times in my life have been shared with the people in my church. We have celebrated the joyous birth of a baby, the landing of the dream job, and the graduation from school. My wife especially loves to have couples over to our home to visit and celebrate what God is doing in our lives.

When we pray together with our church about a worry, it is *subtracted.* Prayer does not always subtract our troubles, but it can subtract our worries. Over the years I have seen God remove the worries from innumerable people through the faithful prayers of fellow believers. Scripture instructs us to "carry each other's burdens" (Galatians 6:2). We do this by taking our trials and troubles in prayer to the One who can meet every need in our lives.

Finally, through the church, blessings are *added* to our lives. The Bible teaches, "Iron sharpens iron, so one man sharpens another (Proverbs 27:17). Parents can draw from parents. In our church, we have many small groups that meet together for Bible study, care time, and share time. When a group has care time, burdens are lifted, and Bible study brings truth that transforms our lives. When a member of the group shares what God is doing, we all learn to apply the biblical truth to our lives.

King Solomon was the wisest king who ever lived (2 Chronicles 9:22). He penned these words: "Two are better than one, because they have a good return for their work: If one falls down, his friend can help him up. But pity the man who falls and has no one to help him up! Also, if two lie down together, they will keep warm. But how can one keep warm alone? Though one may be overpowered, two can defend themselves. A cord of three strands is not quickly broken" (Ecclesiastes 4:9–12). I went camping not long ago and saw King Solomon's principle demonstrated in a different way. As I sat beside the campfire with my family and my friends, I poked the fire with a stick. Whenever I put the stick against the logs in the fire, the stick would ignite and begin to burn. I noticed that the flame would die when I pulled the stick away from the hot coals on the fire. In the fire with the logs, the stick burned bright; but outside of the fire it grew cold. Christians need each other. When we assemble together we can grow spiritually, but if we separate ourselves from a fellowship of believers our faith will grow cold.

At this point in your life are you actively involved in a local church? Are you drawing warmth and encouragement from fellow Christians? Let me frame my point this way: we can no more burn for God by ourselves than a stick can burn outside of a fire. Do not neglect the assembling together with other believers. Being active in a local congregation or gathering is one of the most powerful things you can do to help you introduce your children to Jesus.

Children Learn by Watching

Children are visual learners and learn from watching. Parents can teach children the importance of faith by making gathering for worship with other believers a priority in their lives. As a pastor, I have seen parents drop their children off at church before it starts and then pick them up when it is over. Let me say that this is better than not bringing them at all, but it sends a negative message to the children. Parents who drop their children off at church communicate by their actions that corporate worship is not really all that important. Parents who care about their child's spiritual growth should bring their children to church and worship *with* them.

Ways to Work with the Church

Take your child to church or Sunday school. Church can be a wonderful place of learning and growing for children. I know of a husband and wife who teach Sunday school for three- and four-year-olds. Every Saturday the man telephones every child on their Sunday school class list to make sure he or she will be in church the next day. Each week those little ones look forward to receiving their special phone call. A good Sunday school teacher can make learning about God exciting and fun for children. The Sunday school teachers my children have had have always been a blessing to our family. They have been godly people who have shared insights into God's Word and, more importantly, have shared God's love. Sunday school incorporates spiritual instruction with some of a child's favorite things: crafts, snacks, stories, and songs. Children love the interactive learning they receive there and parents can reinforce that learning by discussing with their children the Bible stories they learn each week.

Show interest in lessons learned at church. Even the most gifted teachers sometimes have difficulty communicating Bible truth in such a way that children can always understand. Children can benefit when parents informally discuss the day's Bible lesson with them. Never assume that a lesson or sermon is over your children's heads or beyond their ability to understand. They may not understand *everything*, but most of the time they will understand *something*. Let your children teach you. Let them ask questions. If your child asks a question for which you don't know the answer, just tell the truth. Once I had a very curious child in our church. She was always asking her mother questions about the Bible. One day she had so many questions that her mother told her to write them all down. The next time I saw the little girl at church she handed me a neatly written, two-page list of questions she wanted answers to. That mother had a great idea: if your child has questions you cannot answer, you can direct them to the pastor or children's minister.

Reinforce good lessons. If a Bible story, craft, or song at church strikes a chord within your child, repeat it at home. Your child will enjoy going through the activity again with a parent. We have many "good lessons" displayed on the refrigerator, the walls and the mirrors of our home. Not long ago I looked at a stack of little crafts my children had done over the years while in Sunday school. Each of the crafts was used to reinforce a lesson my children had learned. Even though they were beginning to clutter my office, I just could not bring myself to throw them away so I started a scrap book for them, and we'll have a record of the good lessons learned. There are many ways you can reinforce those good lessons your children are learning in church.

Let your child sing in a children's choir. Many churches offer a children's choir which meets once a week to teach praise songs and sometimes musicals to children. The value of a children's choir is that the songs teach biblical precepts to the children who sing them. Children love music, and they can easily learn Bible truths and sound doctrine by singing the songs and the great hymns of the faith. When children sing in a choir, parents can take a tape or CD of the music they are learning and play it in the car as the family travels or in the home as they relax or go about their daily chores.

Participate in vacation Bible school and backyard Bible clubs. Each summer children flock to vacation Bible schools and backyard Bible clubs. These events are child favorites because they provide an opportunity for children to sing, do crafts, learn about missions, play, learn Scripture verses, hear Bible stories, and drink Kool-Aid. Your local church could surely use your help as a volunteer worker. If you have not already gotten involved with one of these programs, why not make this your first year—and bring your kids with you.

Parents who depend on the church to influence their children spiritually will impact them one day a week. Parents who partner with the church will help their children develop spiritual beliefs seven days a week. Parents who partner with the church will find a source of help, instruction, and encouragement. The more involved parents are in the life of a church, the better equipped they will be to nurture the spiritual development of their children. I am never surprised when I see the children of godly parents ready to make a faith commitment to Christ at an early age.

Chapter Five

The Physical, Intellectual, and Spiritual Development of Children

And Jesus grew in wisdom and stature, and in favor with God and men. (Luke 2:52)

Every Child Is Different

By reading the second chapter of the Gospel of Luke, parents can gain insight into the childhood of Jesus. Now, it may be more comfortable for us to think of Jesus as an adult in ministry, but the fact is Jesus was once a child and went through all of the struggles of childhood. It is hard for me to comprehend that Jesus was a helpless baby just like my children were. Imagine putting the God who created the universe down for a nap! Yes, Jesus was fully God, but the mystery of the incarnation is that he was as much human as he was divine. Luke 2:43–48 tells us about an episode in Jesus' life:

After the Feast was over, while his parents were returning home, the boy Jesus stayed behind in Jerusalem, but they were unaware of it. Thinking he was in their company, they traveled on for a day. Then they began looking for him among their relatives and friends. When they did not find him, they went back to Jerusalem to look for him. After three days they found him in the temple courts, sitting among the teachers, listening to them and asking them questions. Everyone who heard him was amazed at his understanding and his answers. When his parents saw him, they were astonished. His mother said to him, "Son, why have you treated us like this? Your father and I have been anxiously searching for you."

Jesus, like your child, had a mind of his own. As a parent I can relate somewhat to how Mary and Joseph must have felt as they searched for Jesus. I can just hear them saying, "He has never done anything like this before!" I am sure Mary and Joseph were not calm and collected. After all, they had traveled an entire day before they realized that God's only-begotten son was missing. We cannot be sure, but I think those young parents probably reacted with panic when they could not find Jesus.

Not long ago while on a shopping trip, my four-year-old son decided he was big enough to take a trip of his own. I thought Drew was with my wife, and she thought he was with me, but all the while he was on his very own adventure. Naturally, we assumed the worst—that he had been abducted. We immediately began to fear that someone would harm our precious child, and he would be lost forever. Little did we know that he was having the time of his life! There was a time when this young man would not have struck out on his own; but as he has matured and interacted with adults around him, he has gradually asserted more and more independence. This natural process will continue until he becomes a man. The child Jesus went though this process and, chances are, your child will too.

Scripture teaches that Jesus went through all of the developmental stages your child will go through. Although the Bible does not tell us much about Jesus' childhood, it does tell us that he developed in all areas of his life. Jesus matured physically, intellectually, socially, and spiritually (Luke 2:52). If you, like me, have more than one child, you understand that each child is unique. Yet, despite the obvious differences, each one must go through the same stages of development. An understanding of these developmental stages will help parents better communicate faith truths to their children.

One of the most rewarding experiences of my life was an opportunity I had to coach a first and second grade basketball team. I was given the task of teaching the game to a diverse group of little boys. Some boys had watched basketball; others had never seen a basketball game. Some of the boys were coordinated; and others seemed to be hopelessly at odds with their bodies. The most exciting part of coaching that team was to watch those boys develop as basketball players. During practice I would note where a player was in his development, and at the end of practice would give him a "homework" assignment that would aid in his personal growth as a basketball player. In a few months time I was able to see tremendous progress as my team learned and put into practice skills fundamental to the game of basketball.

There is a spiritual parallel between learning basketball skills and helping our children develop into Christ-followers. Parents need to observe where their children are in their spiritual development, then teach in a developmentally appropriate way.

Stages of Development

The physical, emotional, intellectual, and spiritual development in children is a fairly predictable process. We can know what a child should be capable of doing or understanding at any given stage of development by looking at the normal pattern. Certainly, as we parents seek to nurture spiritual growth in our child, it is helpful to know where she is in her development. For our purposes in this book, we will examine six stages of childhood development. Remember, however, that children are unique and every child develops at his or her own pace. The most important thing to keep in mind is not the age, but the stage of development your child fits into.

Newborn to Two-Year-Olds

Characteristics

Life in this world for children begins with a period of dramatic change, exploration, and discovery. In her book *Joining Children on Their Spiritual Journey*, Katherine Stonehouse describes the incredible change of environment a newborn experiences:

> Before birth the healthy baby's needs are continuously met. Held close in the womb, the child experiences absolute security. Then comes birth; the infant is forcefully pushed in to the big, cold world. The baby faces a crisis; arms and legs stretch out frantically, helplessly, and for the first time there is nothing there. Comfort comes when the little body is again enfolded, this time in a blanket and in the arms of a parent.

Babies live a life of constant discovery. Certainly they require a great deal of one-on-one care and (hopefully) sleep a lot, but they are not lazy by any stretch of the imagination. Think of all the things babies must learn.

His or her entire world is new—every voice, touch, taste, and odor. Babies are learning to associate good and bad with every sense and experience. You and I would have sensory overload if we were thrust into such a drastically new environment.

The first two years are filled with accomplishment. Children learn to roll over, crawl, walk, run, jump, and play games. During this time, toddlers develop from being completely dependent on adult care to asserting their own independence. There is no greater time of progress in the lives of our children than that which occurs between the time of birth and two years of age.

A child also makes tremendous progress in verbal and non-verbal forms of communication during the first two years of life. During this time they develop an extensive vocabulary and sing their first songs. They can listen to and understand simple stories. By the age of two, your child should be saying his or her first prayer to God.

Truths to Teach

In the first year of life children are completely dependent on the care of their parents and the experiences they provide. They learn that certain things are good, some things are cold, and others things are dangerous. This is also a time when they learn who and what to trust. Babies learn that they can call on their parents and have their needs met. Moms and dads can use this time of discovery to teach children that they can trust God. Parents can reinforce this truth by telling them that God is love.

Toddlers love storybooks and coloring books. Parents can use story time and craft time to teach their toddler truths such as *God made me*, *God loves me*, *God wants me to talk to him*, and *We can show our love for Jesus*. For our youngest children, we are the source of their information. What we as parents say becomes a part of their worldview.

When to Start

Many parents and churches wait until children are old enough to walk and talk before they begin spiritual instruction. But, as we have already seen, spiritual in-struction should begin in infancy. It has been said that the best place to start is at the beginning; spiritual instruction should start at the beginning of our life in this world. God's word is not silent when it comes to starting spiritual instruction with our children. Heed the advice of King Solomon: "Train a child in the way he should go, and when he is old he will not turn from it" (Proverbs 22:6). God's word commands us to teach our children: "These commandments that I give you today are to be upon your hearts. *Impress them on your children.* Talk about them when you sit at home and when you walk along the road, when you lie down and when you get up"

(Deuteronomy 6:6–7, emphasis added). Scripture is clear that spiritual instruction starts in childhood.

Take Them to Church

My goal as a parent is to have my children fall in love with our Savior and his church. Two of my children were born in a Baptist hospital and have been in church ever since. One of my greatest achievements as a dad and a pastor is that my children eagerly anticipate going to church every week. In church our children are introduced to a community of faith, Bible teaching, Sunday school, worship, and giving back to God a part of what he has blessed us with. They love church and are growing spiritually because of its influence in their lives. By our participation in the life of our church, our children are able to see that being part of the Church is who we *are* and not just something that we *do* one day a week.

Teachable Moments

Sunday school should be a part of every newborn to two-year-old's spiritual experience. But the most frequent and most effective way to teach simple gospel truth to these little ones is to find teachable moments sprinkled throughout daily life. A shove or a hit from a little friend can become a lesson about forgiveness. In moments of rebellion, parents can teach valuable lessons on obedience that will last a lifetime. Birthdays can become a lesson about the God who made us. Mealtime can be an opportunity to teach that God is our loving provider. Prayer can be easily taught at bedtime as families review the day's events together. Parents should communicate basic truth to children whenever God gives us teachable moments in life.

Memorable Stories

Recently, a friend illustrated for me the power of story-telling with preschoolers. My friend was reading his Bible one day when his young niece saw him and asked what he was reading about. He told his niece the story of the widow's mite in Mark 12. In that story, the widow gives all that she has to God, and the lesson is that we should do the same. My friend said that his sister called him the next week to say that her daughter was so impressed by the story that she was telling everyone she met about the woman who gave all that she had to Jesus. Story-telling communicates spiritual truths to our children in such a way that they will remember them. Perhaps even more importantly, telling spiritual stories will equip our children to pass those truths on to their friends.

My favorite passages of Scripture are narratives. The Bible is largely a collection of narratives. Jesus understood the power of story-telling. He taught in parables—simple stories told to illustrate spiritual truths. In the Gospel, thirty-eight of Jesus' parables are recorded for us. Children of all ages enjoy learning through stories. Parents today can easily find Bible storybooks that are appropriate for children of any age.

Three to Four-Year-Olds

Characteristics

While many people may think of newborn to two-year-olds as being docile, I don't know anyone who would characterize three- and four-year-olds that way. Threes and fours are the reason that child safety caps were invented for chemicals and medications. They can also take credit for the invention of crayons, childproof doorknobs, and those little plastic things you stick in electrical outlets. It is safe to say that three- and four-year-olds are full of energy and curiosity. Children at this age will live life at full speed until suddenly they wear out and fall asleep. They play hard, and they sleep hard. I believe that God designed them this way for the survival of the parents. Where would the parents of preschoolers be without nap time?

Most threes and fours love to talk. By the age of four many preschoolers have a vocabulary in excess of two thousand words. They like to play and are beginning to share toys and take turns with other children. Preschoolers can remember short songs and love to sing. As their motor skills improve, one of the favorite pastimes of the preschooler is building with blocks. Many three- and four-year-olds love to create handicrafts and work puzzles.

Preschool children learn by imitation. In fact, I have seen all three of my children preach a sermon or two. They will watch Mom and Dad carefully, then imitate their behavior or repeat the words they use. I learned early on as a parent not to say things around my children that I did not want the world to know! They will tell on you. Three- and four-year-old children idolize their parents and will imitate both good and bad behavior; so be cautious about the kind of behavior you model in front of them.

Truths to Teach

Three- and four-year-olds are learning to assert their independence. They have learned that crying sometimes gets them what they need and want from their parents, and it is not uncommon see embarrassed parents coping with unruly threes and fours while shopping in the grocery stores. Parents can use this newfound independence teach their children the truth that God wants to have a relationship with them, and they can depend on God to meet their needs. Three- and four-year-olds who are learning about their own independence can learn that they are dependent upon God for everything they have. Up until this time, moms and dads have prayed for their children and even begun to say simple prayers with them. But by the time a child is three-years-old, he will have an adequate vocabulary to express his own thoughts quite well for himself. Moms and dads can encourage their children to talk to God and to tell him whatever is on their hearts. As children come to understand their individuality as separate people apart from mom or dad, parents can begin to teach them that they can have their own relationship with God.

Also keep in mind those teachable moments that arise in the course of daily life, and use them to impart spiritual truth to children of any age. Parents, you can lay a foundation while your child is under the age of six on which you can build a life. As your child grows older, the teaching you put into the moment can become increasingly more abstract and complex. Threes and fours can move from truths such as *God made me* and *God is love*, to W*ho is God?* and *What has God done?* They can understand: *The Bible is God's message to us; We can have a relationship with God; We can be what God wants us to be;* and *We can do what God wants us to do.* Keep track of what your child is learning in Sunday school, and find opportunities to reinforce those lessons at home.

Memorable Stories

Preschoolers never tire of hearing their parents read to them, and rarely will they get bored from hearing the same stories over and over. Just think of how many times your children have seen their favorite cartoon. It would be a shame if our children have seen their favorite cartoon more that they have heard their favorite Bible story. Repetition is a wonderful teacher, and the truths in Bible stories will last their entire lives. Preschoolers love to repeat the Bible stories they have learned. Earlier, we discussed the use of Bible coloring books in the telling of Bible stories from parent to child. This time, try reversing the roles: let your child tell you the story while you color the picture together. David and Goliath, Jonah and the fish, and Daniel in the lion's den are great stories to review with your child.

Five to Six-Year-Olds

Characteristics

Five- and six-year-old children are becoming physically coordinated. Many children by this age are participating in organized athletics and are learning to play together as a team. They can run, skip, and display good eye-hand coordination. Pre-ks and kindergartners can recognize words, print their names, and count. At ages five and six, children are beginning to distinguish truth from fiction. By this age, children are able to understand concepts like *sin* and *forgiveness*. They are beginning to develop a conscience and experience feelings of guilt.

They can begin to understand that God wants to have a relationship with them.

Five- and six-year-olds need to have a growing relationship with God and with others. By the time your child is five, he or she may begin to ask serious questions about spiritual matters. Dads and moms who have been teaching their children about spiritual matters all along can begin the process of teaching them to become followers of Christ and to develop their own relationship with him. They can actively train their children to become committed to God—to launch a lifelong journey with God where they get to know him better through the Bible, prayer, and loving relationships with other Christians. Many children who have been brought up in a Christian home make *faith commitments* during this time in their lives. That is, they express trust in God and his faithfulness, with the intent of turning from sin, looking to God for life direction, and relying on his promise to make them into new people more like Jesus.

Truths to Teach

Children between the ages of five and six readily understand that God watches over us. They can learn about prayer and faith and the relationship between the two. Moms and dads can share their prayer lives with their five- and six-year-old children. They can learn to pray for God's protection in their lives and continue to recognize their dependence on God to meet their physical needs.

Another valuable lesson for five- and six-year-old children is contentment. Parents can teach their children to be content with what they have because God gives us everything we need. They can learn the difference between need and want. They can learn to be happy when they have a lot or when they have a little.

Five- and six-year-olds can grasp the concepts of sin and consequences. They can understand what sin is and that everyone sins—including themselves. They have begun to understand both the concept of guilt and the emotions that are associated with guilt. Parents can teach kids that the penalty for sin is separation from God. With the teaching of guilt and sin parents should teach their children about forgiveness.

Teachable Moments

The older your child becomes, the more teachable moments life will provide. As children interact socially outside the home, they will encounter many life issues through which five- and six-year-olds can learn about forgiveness, prayer, death, and contentment. Parents should pay particular attention in order to capitalize on every opportunity to impact their child's life and shape their worldview.

As children begin elementary school and social inter-actions become increasingly complex, there will be many opportunities to teach about loving, godly relationships.

Don't Take Them for Granted

In some ways parenting appears to begin to be easier the older your children become. They require less personal care from mom and dad. They are able to complete many tasks that mom and dad used to have to do for them. They can even begin to help around the house by performing small chores for their parents.

But with increased independence comes increased autonomy. Children between the ages of five and six will begin to make more and more decisions on their own. As they make these decisions they will make some good decisions that bring reward and some poor decisions which bring bad consequences. Parents of fives and sixes must remain actively engaged with their child.

By age five or six, your child will have his or her own schedule. There will be school, parties, sports, church, and friends. Children at this age can dress themselves and (thanks to the invention of Velcro) they can even put on their own shoes.

This independence can mean that mom and dad pay less attention to what is going in their child's life, especially if that child has younger siblings. Parents should focus on their Pre-ks and kindergartners to see what God is doing in their lives. Often riding in a car will give parents a quiet setting to interact with their children. Bedtime can also be a good quiet time for mom and dad to give their special attention to a child. From time to time, I will single out one of my children for some special time together. During these times we will go places and do things together. I love to take my daughter to the movies. My youngest son likes to go to the hardware store with me, and my middle child, Drew, thinks going to the office together is great. These little excursions give me the opportunity to take their spiritual temperature and to keep up with the things they are learning and dealing with.

Spiritual Exercises

Parents of fives and sixes should encourage their children to continue to enjoy Bible stories and other activities that nurture spiritual growth. By this age children should be encouraged to pray at mealtime and bedtime. Talk about your faith openly with your children, and let them see you having quiet times with God: reading your Bible and praying. Parents can teach their children about serving one another by finding child-sized mission projects to complete. Not long ago a senior lady in our church had hip surgery. My wife taught our children a lesson about serving one another by picking up her mail and taking it to her every day.

Seven to Nine-Year-Olds

Characteristics

Seven to nine-year-old children have left the safety and comfort of home and preschool and have entered the world of elementary school. By this age their brains will be ninety percent of their adult size, and their capacity to think for themselves and understand patterns and processes greater than ever.

Girls and boys usually segregate from each other at this age. Seven to nine-year-olds tend to think that the opposite sex is "gross," and they won't have a lot of playtime interaction with each other. Elementary age children look up to parents, teachers, policemen, firemen, and other authority figures. They love superhero figures.[3]

Elementary age children strive for perfection. They want everything to be exactly right and fair. As they continue to assert their independence, their creativity flourishes. Children at this age still like to be read to, but they also like to read stories on their own. And don't be surprised to find your seven to nine-year-old writing his or her own books

Children in this age range are often impatient. They greatly anticipate special events like Christmas, birthdays, and family vacation. Waiting for a special event can be torture for a seven to nine-year-old.[4]

Truths to Teach

Since children at this age are learning about society and how humans interact, this is a good time for parents to teach children they can obey God by loving one another. They can learn that forgiving others is an act of loving the way God loves us. Parents can also teach children about gossip. They will be tempted to tell everything they know and to talk about other children. Children should be taught not to gossip. When elementary school children encounter authority, parents can reinforce the concept that they honor God when they honor those who are in authority over them. Invariably, first through third graders will experience disappointment and failure as they are growing up. Parents can teach them biblical ways to deal with these negative emotions.

Natural Curiosity

Elementary school age children are curious about the world in which they live. While parents might have a hard time explaining things to preschoolers, they will find that elementary school children not only have inquiring minds, but also are increasingly able to comprehend abstract concepts. Elementary school children are constantly learning how things work. When I was this age, one of my favorite things to do was to take my toys apart so that I could see what made them work. Parents can use this curiosity to their advantage. Mothers and fathers can help these children understand why they believe the things they do.

Teachable Moments

The question "why?" becomes common long before this age, but its importance now increases and provides good opportunities for parents to teach children. Teachable moments will come with questions like: Why do we sing worship songs at church? Why does our family go to church and my friend at school does not? Do pets go to heaven? It will be up to you as a parent to take advantage of these moments when children are open and seeking.

For example, one of my favorite teachable moments with elementary children comes in the form of tattling. Much tattling is plain and simple gossip. I have had occasion to sit down with children and show them several verses from the book of Proverbs about gossip. My favorite is Proverbs 20:19 which states, "A gossip betrays a confidence; so avoid a man who talks too much." Parents can use the undesirable behavior of their children to teach them spiritual lessons.

Parents can also use good behavior to teach spiritual truths to their children. When children love, give, or forgive, parents can use those expressions to reinforce godly behavior in their children. There will be times when our children will stand at the crossroads of a decision. As parents we can use these times to make a lasting spiritual impact on their lives as we walk with them through the spiritual implications of the choices they make.

Spiritual Exercises

Reading is a new and exciting activity for elementary age children. Travel to any Christian bookstore and you will find an ample supply of Christian books for children. There are three different titles I would recommend. First, there is a daily devotional Bible storybook titled, *The Children's Bible In 365 Stories,* by Mary Bachelor. This book has a reading level of age four to eight and works very well for a bedtime storybook.

Thomas Sanders has written a great children's resource titled, *When Can I?* This book is designed for a parent to give to a child when he or she is ready to express faith in Christ. It answers some of the deeper spiritual questions a child will have. This book is written for children, but is a good read for parents as well.

After your child has professed faith in Christ, *I'm a Christian Now,* by Todd Capps and Sherry Shaw, is a fine discipleship resource. This book uses an interactive format to teach children about the meaning of Christian words: baptism, witnessing, the Lord's Supper, the church, and prayer.

Children at this age will be taking a real interest in Christian music. They love to hear other children sing, and they love to sing along with tapes and CDs. One popular resource is a series called *Kids Praise*, which features classic Christian children's songs.

There are some outstanding videos parents can offer children at this age. Big Idea Productions, the makers of *Veggie Tales,* has been consistently producing entertaining, edifying children's videos for ten years. Parents can find an assortment of videos that teach biblical truth at Christian bookstores.

Elementary age children are beginning to explore the world of the internet. There are some decent websites designed for children in this age group. One example is www.kidzap.com. This website features games, music and Bible stories. Another Christian website can be found at www.kidsurf.net. This site features links to child-friendly websites that contain Bible studies, games, help with homework and even a chat room. Christianlink.com/kids is another website that features links which are safe and beneficial to your children. How much you allow your child to surf on the internet is a personal decision, but if you do allow this, please remember to utilize a family filter and monitor all of the websites your child visits.

Ten to Twelve-Year-Olds

Characteristics

Children grow at a rapid rate during these years and will begin to experience great physical changes. During this time both boys and girls become acutely aware that their bodies are developing in ways they have not before. Some children will develop faster than other children, and growth spurts are not uncommon.

All children today are faced with cares and concerns I did not face when I was a child. Between the ages of ten and twelve, I knew nothing of sex or drugs. Evil has been in the world since the beginning, but it no longer hides in the night. Today older elementary age children face cares, worries, and temptations that were reserved for adolescence in years gone by.

By the time a child is twelve, he will be asserting his independence and his preferences more than ever before. Preteens develop a personal style in the way they dress, the games they play, the music they listen to, and the friends they keep. In the coming teen years, parents will have less and less influence on their children, therefore it is imperative that parents help older elementary age children know how to make good decisions in life.

Take Them to Church

Children's church and Sunday school are effective

ways to minister to older elementary children. These programs give kids the opportunity to experience worship which targets their specific developmental level. Worship services for older elementary children should include praise music, drama, video, games, crafts, and Bible stories. In addition to Children's church, many churches offer discipleship, Scripture memory, and missions programs for elementary children. Programs like Awana, Team Kid, Royal Ambassadors, and Mission Kids provide age-appropriate Bible study opportunities for elementary children.

Summer Camp

Summer camp is a fun way to sow spiritual seeds into the lives of ten- to twelve-year-old children. Each year there are Christian camps organized all over the country for elementary age children. Some churches organize their own children's camps; there are also denominational, non-denominational camps, and excellent camps organized by parachurch organizations like the Navigators or Young Life. Summer camps provide preteens with the opportunity to live for a week without video games, television, MP3 players, and a million other distractions they encounter on a daily basis. As the distractions are taken from the children, they are challenged to think about weighty matters of morality and spirituality.

Chapter Six

How to Know When Your Child Is Ready

Come, my children, listen to me; I will teach you the fear of the LORD. (Psalm 34:11)

A Legacy of Faith

Every Christian parent prays for their children to place their faith in Christ as their own Savior. My favorite testimonies of faith are those in which a person makes a faith commitment to Christ at an early age and lives faithfully for God as they mature. Many powerful, successful, and famous people became Christ-followers as children. In each of the following examples parents were able to pass their faith on to their children.

The late W. A. Criswell professed faith in Christ at the age of ten. Among his great accomplishments are the founding of Criswell College in Dallas, Texas, and the pastoring of the First Baptist Church of Dallas, Texas, for half a century. He also held the office of president of the Southern Baptist Convention for two terms.

S. Truett Cathy is the founder and CEO of Chick-fil-A, Inc., a company which has over 700 restaurants across the country. Cathy professed his faith in Jesus Christ at the age of twelve. In a time when so many corporate CEOs have been exposed as corrupt, Mr. Cathy stands out as a shining example of how a successful Christian business-man should live.

Television news personality Deborah Norville accepted Christ when she was fifteen-years-old. She has influenced millions of viewers by being open about her faith in Christ.

Dr. Jack Graham is the pastor of the 20,000 member Prestonwood Baptist Church in Plano, Texas. He recently served two terms as the president of the Southern Baptist Convention. He is the host of the television program *The Baptist Hour* and has authored several books. Dr. Graham made a faith commitment to Christ at the tender age of six.

Contemporary Christian artist Amy Grant accepted Jesus as her Savior at the age of thirteen. Among her many achievements are five Grammy awards and seventeen Dove awards. She has sold more than eighteen million records worldwide.

Jimmy Carter, the thirty-ninth president of the United States, was born again at age ten. He made the phrase "born again" a popular term for someone who has become a Christian. Notable among his many contributions to society is his work with Habitat for Humanity and his efforts to bring peace in our world. In 2002 he was awarded the Nobel Peace Prize for his efforts to find peaceful solutions to international conflicts, to advance democracy and human rights, and to promote economic and social development.

Dr. Jerry Rankin is the president of the International Mission Board of the Southern Baptist Convention. Dr. Rankin made a profession of faith when he was ten-years-old. Under his leadership the International Mission Board has grown to over five thousand missionaries worldwide.

Age of Accountability

For centuries the church has struggled with the question, When is a child accountable to God for their salvation? This is known as the "age of accountability." We can define the age of accountability as the point in time when a child has the ability to reason and choose right from wrong and to accept or reject the gospel.

Some Christian parents assume that a child becomes accountable at twelve years of age. This probably stems from the Jewish practice of *bar mitzvah*—at thirteen, a boy is considered an adult (a girl at twelve) and responsible for his or her moral and religious choices. The Catholic Church teaches that a child reaches the "age of reason" at or around age seven. In truth, the age of accountability is not so much about age as it is about ability to reason.

As a pastor I have had opportunities to have spiritual conversations with many children over the years. I can say from personal experience that every child is different. Children develop physically, mentally, and spiritually at different rates. One child may be ready to make a faith commitment to Christ at age six, while another child may not be spiritually ready to commit his or her life to Christ until he or she is much older.

The Bible does not teach directly on the subject, but some passages of Scripture can give us guidance about the concept of the age of accountability. We know from the book of 2 Samuel that babies are not held accountable to God. King David's baby son had become ill and died. David had mourned and prayed for the baby while the child was still alive. Yet after he died, David returned to his normal lifestyle. In 2 Samuel 12:22–23, David told his servants, "While the child was still alive, I fasted and wept. I thought, 'Who knows? The LORD may be gracious to me and let the child live.' But now that he is dead, why should I fast? Can I bring him back again? I will go to him, but he will not return to me." David took comfort in knowing that his son would be waiting for him in the presence of God even though the son had neither an understanding of good and evil nor an opportunity to choose to follow God's life.

Isaiah 7:15 implies that there is a point in time when a child has the opportunity to refuse evil and choose good: "He will eat curds and honey when he knows enough to reject the wrong and choose the right." Young children learn at an early age the difference between good and bad behavior. However, there comes a time in a child's life when he has the capacity to rationally choose what is good to do or what is bad to do. Parents experience this when they hold an older child to a higher standard of behavior than they do a younger child.

Jesus said, "Let the little children come to me, and do not hinder them, for the kingdom of God belongs to such as these" (Luke 18:16). Children do not have to be taught how to sin. They come by it naturally. They do bad things from time to time, but they also lose something as they mature. Little children have a certain innocence and faith. But when a child comes to the age in which he or she begins to choose to do evil instead of good, they have come to the age of accountability.

How a Child Begins a Spiritual Journey

When children begin to express interest in having a relationship with Jesus, they will most likely begin by asking some deep questions prompted by things they have experienced. Children who go to school will meet others with a wide variety of beliefs which may provoke questions for discussion. Children who attend church will see the church celebrating baptism and the Lord's Supper and will often want to participate themselves.

In my ministry, I have found that a child's interest in baptism and the Lord's Supper can be a wonderful teaching opportunity. As children ask questions about these events, they will learn that they are directly connected to having a relationship with Jesus Christ. They must be a Christian to do these things. Initially, children may be interested just to be like everyone else. But as they begin to understand the meaning of these ordinances, they will often ask deeper questions. If this doesn't happen, do not be afraid to initiate a conversation with your child about the meaning of these spiritual activities.

The Lord's Supper

Jesus gave us the practices of communion and baptism as teaching tools and visual lessons about his sacrifice on the cross. In 1 Corinthians 11:26 Paul says, "For whenever you eat this bread and drink this cup, you proclaim the Lord's death until he comes." Each time we celebrate the Lord's supper we proclaim to each other and all who are in attendance what Jesus has done for us through his death and resurrection. Children can learn that Christians celebrate the Lord's Supper to remember that Jesus died for our sins and that he will one day return for those who belong to him.

Baptism

In Jesus' last days on this earth, he commanded his followers to "go and *make disciples* of all nations, *baptizing* them in the name of the Father and of the Son and of the Holy Spirit, and teaching them to obey everything I have commanded you. And surely I am with you always, to the very end of the age" (Matthew 28:19–20, emphasis added). In this Great Commission to the disciples, Jesus commanded them to do two things: to make disciples and to baptize. As the disciples shared the good news about what Jesus had done, they baptized new believers. Baptism identified the new converts with the disciples. Today we continue to identify new Christians with the church through baptism.

Not only does baptism identify a Christ-follower with the church, but it also demonstrates the essence of the gospel—the death and resurrection of Jesus—and becomes a powerful teaching tool for the church. Parents can teach their children the gospel message of Christ by explaining the meaning of baptism. Children can learn that baptism is a symbol of the death, burial, and resurrection of Jesus. Colossians 2:12 says you have been "buried with him in baptism and raised with him through your faith in the power of God, who raised him from the dead." They can also learn that a person is identified with Jesus and the church through baptism.

Parents can use the meaning and importance of these two ordinances to impart spiritual truth to their children. When children begin to ask questions about the Lord's Supper or baptism, they are beginning to express real spiritual interest. Parents should take advantage of this opportunity and explain the meaning of these ordinances.

What They Must Understand to Be Ready

I have been approached on more than one occasion by a parent who has said, "My child is asking questions about salvation, but how do I know if he is really ready?" This is a natural reaction for a parent of a young child who wants to make a faith commitment to Christ. In fact, I too have been in this position. Christian parents should keep a couple of things in mind when their young child begins to express interest in having a personal relationship with Jesus Christ.

First, parents should not be surprised. They have been preparing their child for this decision from the day of birth. They have sung songs about the love of God and have prayed for salvation. They have colored pictures, gone to church, read the Bible, and done dozens of other things to bring this child to Jesus. Congratulations, Mom and Dad! You have been successful. You, just like the parents in Luke, chapter eighteen, have brought your child to Jesus.

A second thing to keep in mind is that although your child does not need to know everything at once, there are some things he or she must know and understand in order to enter a relationship with God through Jesus.

God loves them and has a special plan for them. 1 John 4:10 states: "This is love: not that we loved God, but that he loved us and sent his Son as an atoning sacrifice for our sins." Salvation starts with God. It starts with the fact that God loves us and desires a relationship with us. John 3:16 tells us about the plan that God has for our children: "For God so loved the world that he gave his one and only Son, that whoever believes in him shall not perish but have eternal life." God's plan for our children is to give them eternal life.

Sin separates us from God. "But your iniquities have separated you from your God; your sins have hidden his face from you, so that he will not hear" (Isaiah 59:2). "For the wages of sin is death, but the gift of God is eternal life in Christ Jesus our Lord" (Romans 6:23). Death is eternal separation from God, and separation from God is hell.

Sin is breaking God's law. One child described sin as doing something that makes God sad. Sin begins with a rebellious attitude but almost always manifests itself in an action—doing something we should not have done or neglecting to do something we should have done. Ultimately, sin's rebellion against God brings a need for forgiveness into our lives. Children who understand sin know that they need someone to save them from sin and its penalty.

Everyone has sinned. "For all have sinned and fall short of the glory of God" (Romans 3:23). In my experience, children who are ready to express their faith understand that sin is doing something that God does not want us to do. Children who understand sin know that they themselves have sinned and can name an example of a sinful attitude or action they have committed.

A couple brought their six-year-old boy to my office one day. They told me that their son had prayed and invited Jesus into his heart and now wanted to be baptized. I began to talk to him about his salvation. I asked him if he knew what sin was. He gave a good Sunday school answer: "When we do something God does not want us to do." I then asked him who has sinned. He replied, "Everyone has sinned." I asked, "Have *you* ever sinned?" Looking at his parents, he grinned and told of something he had done for which he blamed his little sister. I asked him why that was wrong, and he told me that it was wrong because he had lied. This six-year-old had a clear understanding of both the concept and the practice of sin.

Jesus is God's son and our salvation. Children must understand who Jesus is: he is God's son. God loves us and gave his son, Jesus, for the forgiveness of our sins: "This is how much God loved the world: He gave his Son, his one and only Son. And this is why: so that no one need be destroyed; by believing in him, anyone can have a whole and lasting life" (John 3:16 THE MESSAGE). Most of all, they need to understand that Jesus is "the way and the truth and the life" and that no one comes to the Father any way except through Jesus (John 14:6). Through Jesus we can have forgiveness of sins and salvation. Children must understand that faith in Jesus is the only way anyone can be saved.

Jesus died on the cross for us. Children must have an understanding of what Jesus did on the cross before they can be saved. "But God demonstrates his own love for us in this: While we were still sinners, Christ died for us" (Romans 5:8). Children need to believe that Jesus died on the cross to pay for *their* sin, and he rose from the grave. "If you confess with your mouth, 'Jesus is Lord,' and believe in your heart that God raised him from the dead, you will be saved" (Romans 10:9). Children must also realize that they need to place their faith in Jesus and live for him. It is one thing to have a belief that Jesus is the Savior, but it is an entirely different thing to own the knowledge that we are to live our lives to serve him. This principle is clearly taught in 2 Corinthians 5:15: "And he died for all, that those who live should no longer live for themselves but for him who died for them and was raised again." Becoming a Christ-follower means giving our lives to Jesus just as he gave his life for us. Our Lord calls children and adults alike to discipleship.

The Determining Factor

We have talked at length of teachable moments. Everyday life will provide openings for parents to discern the spiritual maturity of their children. As a parent, one of those moments came to me when my oldest child asked me when she could invite Jesus into her heart. The first time she asked that question she did not yet understand what it meant to commit her life to Christ, but it did open the door for me to share the gospel with her. Every child is different, and these opportunities will come in different ways and at different times. Parents, when they do come, be ready to take advantage of the opportunities.

How To Know

The best way for a parent to determine whether or not their child is ready to make a faith commitment to Christ is to ask the questions:

Who is Jesus?

What is sin?

What did Jesus do?

How can we go to heaven?

Are you ready to live for Jesus?

Parents should also ask follow-up questions to these listed. If a child demonstrates an understanding of these core truths, he or she is ready to profess a real faith in Christ. After Mom and Dad have explained salvation and prayed with their child, they may want to make an appointment with a pastor or children's minister to share the good news and investigate the next steps in the discipleship process.

Chapter Seven

How to Lead Your Child to Christ

He then brought them out and asked, 'Sirs, what must I do to be saved?' (Acts 16:30)

The Day Has Come

When you determine that God has been dealing with your child and that he or she is ready to express their own faith in God as a believer in Christ, then it is time to share a presentation of the gospel. You don't need a seminary degree to share the gift of salvation with your child. I love to pray with the children in my church as they invite Jesus to come into their hearts to be their Lord and Savior, but what I enjoy the most is when parents tell me how they have been the ones who helped their child formalize his relationship to God through Jesus. As we have previously seen, it is the parents' privilege, not the pastor's privilege, to lead their child to Christ.

The day your child makes a faith commitment to Christ is the single most important day in his or her life.

Some parents may be intimidated by the gravity of this experience for their child, but they should not be. It is my desire in this chapter to prepare parents to lead their children to Christ and my joy to know that many parents will indeed have the opportunity to use the techniques found in these pages to bring their children to Jesus, just as the parents did in Luke, chapter eighteen. It is my prayer that every parent who reads this book will have the joy of hearing their children pray to invite Jesus into their hearts.

A Little Help

I have shared the gospel with children in the church sanctuary, in classrooms, in their homes, in my office, and even outdoors. Out of my experience, I'd like to offer a little common sense advice that will help moms and dads share the gospel effectively with their children.

Limiting distractions in the environment will help parents share and children learn. It's no secret that children often demonstrate short attention spans. Limiting distractions will help them focus on the gospel. Today many parents have difficulty giving their children their undivided attention. We allow the trappings of work and culture to come between us and the development of our children. Phones, beepers, radios, computers, and televisions should be turned off. Siblings can also cause distractions in the home when parents are trying to share the gospel with a child. Moms and dads cannot give a child their complete attention if they are tending to a younger or older sibling.

As parents we should attempt to recreate the atmosphere that must have surrounded the parents in Luke, chapter eighteen. I can imagine that they were excited about the opportunity to take their child to Jesus. I can also imagine that they were reverent and respectful as they told their children who Jesus was. Parents should strive to be excited and enthusiastic, but we should also be reverent as we tell our children about Jesus.

Parents should not be overbearing as they share the gospel with their child. On more than one occasion I have encountered what I call the "coach" parent. Some parents want their child to follow Christ so badly that they coach their child all the way through the decision process. They fear their child will not answer spiritual questions in the right way, so they answer questions for them, or they lead their child to the right answers to the questions that are asked about spiritual matters. Parents should not answer questions for their children nor lead them to the right answer. If a child is ready to express faith in Christ, coaching will not be necessary. It may be hard for a parent to release a child and trust her to put her spiritual beliefs into her own words. Please resist the urge to finish her sentences for her.

Sometimes children profess faith in Christ because they feel pressured into doing so. Parents should understand that the child's faith belongs to the child. A parent who pressures a child into making a public declaration of faith in Jesus could turn their child off to having a genuine relationship with Christ in the future. Pressuring a child into a faith that is not his own can create resentment that will last for a lifetime. As badly as we want to pass on our spiritual beliefs, we cannot force him to believe as we do. We must trust God do the work of drawing our children. Children should never express faith in Christ because they feel that it is expected of them.

While some parents mistakenly pressure their children, other parents use bribery. Parents should not bribe their children in order to get them to make a commitment to Christ. Children should not be promised a reward if they will pray to invite Christ into their hearts and be baptized. I think their decision should be celebrated, but any gifts to commemorate this important occasion should be a surprise to the child.

If a parent is sharing with a child and he or she isn't ready to become a Christian, the parent should back off of the subject and approach it again at another time. Many parents would be tempted at this point to use guilt to manipulate the child into making a commitment to Christ. This should never be the case. The parent should end the time by praying for God to make himself real in the child's life and for God's will to be done. After all, a great deal of Christian parenting is trusting our children to the will and care of our heavenly Father.

When sharing with a child, parents should avoid theological terms. The conversation should be on the child's level using words he or she understands. Children are literal thinkers, so parents should avoid using symbolic terms like salvation, faith, born again, repentance, and lordship without adequate explanation. Parents should not assume that their children have a full understanding of the words we use to express our faith. When sharing the gospel with your children, keep your vocabulary simple. There will be plenty of time for theology lessons in the future.

When presenting the gospel to younger children, it is important to stay on the subject. If the subject should change, it may be necessary to bring short attention spans back to the topic at hand. If it is too difficult to stay on subject, it may be best to try again at a later time with fewer distractions. It would be better to open a spiritual dialogue at another time than force a commitment that is not real.

A final piece of advice comes in the area of clarifying a child's motivation for making a faith commitment to Christ. The parents in my church usually see an increase in spiritual interest from their children whenever we baptize someone or celebrate communion. As their spiritual interest increases, so will the number of questions they will ask. Every year our church will sponsor a vacation Bible school, and almost every year our church will see children baptized as a result of faith commitments made there. Children who have not yet been baptized will want to be when they see their friends being baptized. It is the nature of children to want to do what they see their friends doing. As pastor I am careful to make sure that children are not expressing faith in Christ because their friends are. Peer pressure is not the right motivation for a child to publicly express faith in Christ. I encourage parents to use these kinds of opportunities to talk to their children about what it means to be a Christian.

Presenting the Gospel

It has been my experience that a very effective way to communicate the gospel to children is to use gospel tracts designed and written specifically with children in mind. Have you ever noticed that many of the characters in television cartoons are children? Preteen television shows feature other preteens; teen shows feature teens. There are many good gospel tracts written for children that feature children. Campus Crusade has a tract titled *The Four Spiritual Laws for Children*, and the North American Mission Board of the Southern Baptist Convention has one called *God's Special Plan*.

Although I recommend the use of booklets or tracts to lead children to faith in Christ, I recognize that there are other effective means of sharing the gospel with children. One of the most creative ways to share with children is a presentation called an *Evangecube*. The Evangecube is an unfolding puzzle that presents the gospel in a colorful and creative way. Children love puzzles, and the Evangecube is a sure way to capture your child's attention as you share the gospel story with her.

Another tool parents can use to present the gospel to their children is the *salvation bracelet*. This bracelet consists of a leather string and a series of beads. It can be simple or elaborate. A simple salvation bracelet should contain a black bead which symbolizes our sins; a red bead which symbolizes the blood of Jesus; a blue bead for baptism; a white bead symbolizing forgiveness; a green bead symbolizing Christian growth; a gold bead for the promise of heaven; and a seventh, purple bead that is a reminder that we are to worship God. Parents can purchase the materials necessary to make the salvation bracelet at any hobby store. Mom and Dad can share the gospel with their child as they make the salvation bracelets together. The bracelet will serve as a reminder to both parent and child of the commitment to Christ that was made.

On several occasions I have used a gift Bible to share the gospel with someone. Parents can purchase a special Bible to be used to lead their child to Christ. When the time is right, a parent can take the special Bible and go through the plan of salvation with their child. As dad and mom lead their child through the Scriptures, the child can underline or highlight the Bible verses used. You can write the list of Scriptures in the order they are used in the front of the Bible. After your child has prayed to receive Christ, you can sign and date the Bible. The Bible will serve as a reminder of the faith commitment your child has made.

Prayer

After your child has demonstrated an understanding of the Gospel, it is time to encourage him to express his faith in Christ through prayer. The Bible teaches, "Everyone who calls on the name of the Lord will be saved " (Romans 10:13). We call on the name of the Lord through prayer. Prayer is simply talking to God. As a person prays a prayer for salvation, there are a few things that they should tell God in their prayer. The prayer should be a confession of the truths that have been established in the gospel presentation. A prayer for salvation can go something like this:

> "Dear God, I know I am a sinner; please forgive me. I believe Jesus died on the cross for my sins and that he rose again. Jesus, please come into my heart and be my Lord and savior. Today I give my life to you. Amen."

Chapter Eight

Making Salvation Memorable

I have been reminded of your sincere faith, which first lived in your grandmother Lois and in your mother Eunice and, I am persuaded, now lives in you also. (2 Timothy 1:5)

A Biblical Principle

The book of 2 Timothy was written to Timothy, a young pastor serving the church in Ephesus, by the apostle Paul. Paul had been Timothy's spiritual mentor and considered his relationship with Timothy so special that he called Timothy "his son" (2 Timothy 1:2). Being the pastor of the church at Ephesus would have been a challenging task for a seasoned minister, much less a young man like Timothy. Before Paul gave Timothy instruction as to what to do as pastor, he reminded Timothy of his faith: "I have been reminded of your sincere faith, which first lived in your grandmother Lois and in your mother Eunice and, I am persuaded, now lives in you also" (2 Timothy 1:5).

Not only did Paul remind him of his faith, but also how his faith came about. In the spiritual battles that were to take place in Timothy's life, he could draw strength from the knowledge that his faith was his own and that it had been passed on to him by people who loved and cared deeply for him. No doubt Timothy was encouraged to remember that he was genuinely a part of a community of faith. As our children face the difficulties of life, it will be helpful for them as well to know they are not alone.

If you are like me, you want to insulate your children from the bad things of life and shelter them from everything unpleasant. But reality is that things will not always be easy for our children. As they go through life, they will face peer pressure, doubt, fear, worry, distraction, discouragement, temptation, and many other forces that could threaten their spiritual growth. Like Paul, parents today can strengthen their children by reinforcing the memories they have of their faith commitment. Making their salvation experience memorable will give them comfort in difficult times and help them to make good choices in life.

Memorials

We can make salvation memorable for our children by creating a memorial that will commemorate the day they expressed faith in Christ. Throughout the Bible, God's people have used memorials to remember the important events in their spiritual lives. Generally speaking a spiritual memorial is an object or an event that celebrates and reminds us of a time when we have encountered God. A spiritual memorial reminds us of something that God has done for us.

One of the more familiar biblical accounts of a memorial comes in the book of Joshua as God's chosen people finally enter into the promised land after many years of wandering in the wilderness.

When the whole nation had finished crossing the Jordan, the LORD said to Joshua, "Choose twelve men from among the people, one from each tribe, and tell them to take up twelve stones from the middle of the Jordan from right where the priests stood and to carry them over with you and put them down at the place where you stay tonight."

So Joshua called together the twelve men he had appointed from the Israelites, one from each tribe, and said to them, "Go over before the ark of the LORD your God into the middle of the Jordan. Each of you is to take up a stone on his shoulder, according to the number of the tribes of the Israelites, to serve as a sign among you. In the future, when your children ask you, 'What do these stones mean?' tell them that the flow of the Jordan was cut off before the ark of the covenant of the LORD. When it crossed the Jordan, the waters of the Jordan were cut off. These stones are to be a memorial to the people of Israel forever."

So the Israelites did as Joshua commanded them. They took twelve stones from the middle of the Jordan, according to the number of the tribes of the Israelites, as the LORD had told Joshua; and they carried them over with them to their camp, where they put them down. Joshua set up the twelve stones that had been in the middle of the Jordan at the spot where the priests who carried the ark of the covenant had stood. And they are there to this day. (Joshua 4:1–9)

Using stones from the River Jordan, the Israelites created a memorial so that they, and their descendants, would remember what God had done for them on that day. Objects and ceremonies have great power to remind us of God. When we remember what he has done for us, we are strengthened spiritually. There are some things we can do as parents to help our children remember the most important spiritual event of their lives.

A Spiritual Birthday

The day a child becomes a Christian is his or her spiritual birthday. Jesus spoke of a person entering into a relationship with God through himself as being *born again*. "In reply Jesus declared, 'I tell you the truth, no one can see the kingdom of God unless he is born again'" (John 3:3). If you understand salvation through the metaphor of birth, then it makes sense to celebrate a spiritual birth as much as you would a physical birth.

Birthdays are celebrated to keep track of age, commemorate that very special occasion (birth), and to let the birthday boy or girl know how they are special and loved. The purpose of celebrating a spiritual birthday is the same.

While it is not essential to remember the day and year one makes a faith commitment, there is great value in remembering the date. In the coming years the date of a spiritual birthday will help serve as a spiritual anchor in the life of your child. By celebrating the date that your child placed trust in Christ, parents give her confidence in her faith commitment.

First Confessions

When a child makes a commitment to Christ, he should be encouraged to share that decision with the important people in his life. Sunday school teachers, grandparents, aunts and uncles can share the joy and excitement of the moment with you and your child. These first confessions of newfound faith will add confidence to your child's spiritual attitude.

Encouraging children to tell their spiritual story right

away will set a valuable pattern of faith-sharing in their lives. Moms and dads should teach their children how to tell other people about their faith. This is a time when coaching by a parent is not only allowed, but encouraged.

A salvation story or testimony should contain three parts. The first part of a testimony usually tells about our life before we came to Christ. For your child, this part of the testimony could include a little background information on his or her spiritual life and some of the events and feelings that led to making a faith commitment to Christ.

The second part of a testimony is the story of how your child came to profess faith in Christ. This part of the testimony should contain the what, when, and where of the salvation experience. For example, the second part of my salvation experience took place in a preacher's living room on a spring night as a teenager.

The final and shortest part of a salvation testimony for a child is what life has been like since expressing faith in Christ. Children should share how they felt after they asked Jesus into their heart and tell about how God has been at work in their lives.

Baptism

Baptism is in itself a beautiful reminder of our salvation experience. It is a visible picture of the death, burial, and resurrection of Jesus. The baptism of our children should make salvation more memorable in their lives. Believers from New Testament times until today practice baptism as a symbol of the spiritual change that has come in our lives through faith in Jesus Christ. Parents can use baptism to remind their child of the commitment they have made to be a Christ-follower.[5]

A Tangible Memory

In our homes we keep souvenirs that remind us of the great times we have had, the meaningful things we have done, and the awesome places we have been in our lives. Our memories are fortified and enhanced by the things that remind us of these experiences. Some parents make salvation a tangible memory by buying a special book or Bible to mark the occasion.

One of my greatest treasures is a Bible my Sunday school teacher gave me to mark the occasion of my joining the church. My special Bible is an inexpensive, black bonded-leather, King James Version Bible. I have not read from this Bible in years, but it serves as a memory-marker for one of the most important events in my life. When a child comes to Christ, his or her parent can give a gift that will serve as a memory, commemorate this special event, and aid in their spiritual growth. A little thought about your child and his or her spiritual needs can lead you to a gift that will be cherished for years to come.

Godparents

Some faith traditions name godparents at the time of a child's spiritual milestone experience such as baptism. A godparent is someone who is named as a sponsor for that child and often maintains close, almost familial relationships with a godchild. One of the primary responsibilities of a godparent is to provide spiritual support for both the parent and the child. Godparents serve as witnesses to the mutual faith they and the child have in God.

The practice of naming godparents to share in the spiritual lives of our children is a positive practice that should be considered by parents from all denominational backgrounds. Many protestant denominations practice baby dedications. The concept behind dedicating a baby is similar to that of naming a godparent. As a mother and father dedicate a baby, the church, as a family of faith, commits to participate in the spiritual upbringing of a child. Godparents make a similar but more personal commitment.

John even though he had no sins to confess or repent.

After Jesus died on the cross and rose from the grave, he spent some quality teaching time with his disciples and gave them (the first church) instructions to carry out after he was gone: "Go and make disciples of all nations, baptizing them in the name of the Father and of the Son and of the Holy Spirit" (Matthew 28:19). Baptism is not necessary for salvation, but it is necessary so that one can be an obedient follower of Christ. Parents can teach children to be obedient to the teachings of Christ by encouraging them to follow their commitment to Christ with baptism. Baptism is perhaps the most powerful symbol we as Christians may have concerning salvation; therefore, parents should make every effort to make the event memorable and special for children.

Chapter Nine

Making Disciples of Your Children

Therefore go and make disciples of all nations, baptizing them in the name of the Father and of the Son and of the Holy Spirit, and teaching them to obey everything I have commanded you. And surely I am with you always, to the very end of the age. (Matthew 28:19–20)

In the Image of the Father

I can see my image in all three of my children. Of the three, my middle child probably looks the most like me, but my oldest child's personality is the closest to mine. I enjoy it when people tell me my children are just like me. I believe that our heavenly Father also wants to see his image in our lives and in the lives of our children. He wants to see his image in each of us. God's Word tells us, "So God created man in his own image, in the image of God he created him; male and female he created them" (Genesis 1:27). Romans 8:29 reaffirms God's desire to see his spiritual children conform to his image: "For those God foreknew he also predestined to be conformed to the likeness of his Son." Ultimately the job of making disciples of our children can be described as transforming our children into the image of our heavenly Father.

Our deoxyribonucleic acid, or DNA, determines to a great deal who we are. Humor columnist Dave Barry has said, "The information encoded in your DNA determines your unique biological characteristics, such as sex, eye color, age, and social security number." I am not so sure about the social security number, but your DNA does determine much of how you look, what you like, and how you respond to life. When our children place their faith in Jesus, God gives them a brand new spiritual DNA. DNA comes from a sharing of life between two parents. When our children make a faith commitment to Christ, God shares his life with them through the Holy Spirit. It is our job as parents to disciple our children to allow those Christ-like characteristics to overtake who they were so they can become who God wants them to be.

The Great Commission

The Christian life is more than a one-time decision to follow Christ. After his resurrection as Jesus was about to return to heaven, he told the first church (his disciples), "Therefore go and make disciples of all nations . . .

teaching them to obey everything I have commanded you" (Matthew 28:19–20). It is not enough for parents to lead their children to the cross; we must teach them to be followers of Christ daily—"If anyone would come after me, he must deny himself and take up his cross daily and follow me" (Luke 9:23).

It is vital for Christian parents to understand that Jesus never commanded the church to get people to pray a prayer. If you listen to some evangelists, you might believe that the work for parents is over when their child prays and invites Jesus into his or her heart. This practice leads to intellectual assent, but not to discipleship. A disciple is a learner or follower of Christ. Our biblical role as parents is to teach our children to believe in Jesus and what he has done and to become *lifelong disciples*.

The Transition

When our children pray to receive Christ into their hearts, they go from being the *target* to being the *arrow*. Up until this time in their lives they have been the target of ministry; now they can begin to be ministers. While we used to pray for the spiritual rebirth of our children, we may now begin to pray that our children will yield their lives to the Savior and become like him in every way. Making disciples of our children means a transition from teaching them *about* Jesus to teaching them to *follow* Jesus. Parents can make disciples of their children by teaching them how to pray, share their faith, have a devotional life, and worship.

Teach Them How to Pray

Prayer is talking to God. If you think about it, praying is a lot like writing a letter to God. In many prayers, as in letters, there is a greeting, a body, and a closing. Dads and moms can sit down with a pencil and a piece of paper and teach their children how to pray.

Every letter starts with a greeting. If you were to begin a letter to me you would start by writing "Dear Brian." When Jesus taught his disciples to pray he started the model prayer with the greeting, "Our Father in heaven" (Matthew 6:9). Children can begin their prayer with a greeting to God. In our home our children start their prayers by saying "Dear God."

The second part of a letter is the body. The body contains the purpose for writing the letter. It contains good wishes, requests and information. Children can tell or write to God what they wish in the body of a prayer. The body of Jesus' model prayer included words of worship and requests for God's provision and forgiveness; he also prayed for God's direction and protection. I encourage my children to tell God whatever they want to tell him. I think it is important to teach children that God cares and wants to hear what is on our hearts.

The final part of a letter is called the closing. Jesus closed his model prayer with "Amen" (Matthew 6:13 KJV). In our home we teach our children to close their prayers by saying "in Jesus' name, Amen." Although there are no prayers in the Bible that end with the phrase *in Jesus' name,* it is clearly a biblical concept. In John's gospel Jesus stated, "You may ask me for anything *in my name*, and I will do it" (John 14:14). Jesus also said, "In that day you will no longer ask me anything. I tell you the truth, my Father will give you whatever you *ask in my name*" (John 16:23). When we pray in the name of Jesus we are declaring our relationship to him and praying according to his power and authority, not our own. The smallest child praying in the name of Jesus has the ear of his or her Father in Heaven.

Learning to pray is ultimately learning to trust God in every circumstance in our lives. When we take our joy, sorrow, want, intercession, and need to our heavenly Father, we share our life with him and thus grow closer to him. Teaching our children to pray is teaching them to know God, not just know about God.

Teach Them to Share Their Faith

The book of Matthew records Jesus telling the church to "go and make disciples" (Matthew 28:19). Just before Jesus ascended into heaven, he told the church, "You will be my witnesses in Jerusalem, and in all Judea and Samaria, and to the ends of the earth" (Acts 1:8). As Christians go into the world, they go as Jesus' witnesses. Christian parents must teach their children to go into the world as his witnesses.

Evangelism

When we think of Jesus' command to "Go make disciples," we think of evangelism. In its simplest form, evangelism is demonstrating how people can enter into an eternal relationship with God. Children can participate in evangelism by praying for their classmates, friends, and relatives. Parents who teach their children to pray for non-Christian friends and family teach them about the urgency of evangelism.

One of the most effective forms of evangelism is telling friends about Jesus. In John 4, Jesus met a Samaritan woman at a well. After she confessed that Jesus was the Messiah, she went back to town to find her friends and take them to meet Jesus. Children can participate in evangelism by telling their friends about Jesus too.

Another method of personal evangelism is to bring someone to hear someone else speak about Jesus. In Acts 10, a Roman soldier named Cornelius sent his servants to bring the apostle Peter to his home to speak to him, his friends, and his family about Jesus. By bringing his friends together to hear Peter tell about Jesus, Cornelius participated in evangelism. Parents can teach their children to do evangelism by encouraging them to bring their non-Christian friends to church, Sunday school, or youth group.

Jesus' commandment to "Go make disciples" applies to all of his followers—no matter what size they are. As Christian parents our responsibility is doubled. We are to be Jesus' witnesses everywhere we go, and we are to lead our children to be his witnesses as well.

Love God and Love Others

Jesus spent three years with his disciples before he sent them out. He knew that they needed to spend time not only listening to him, but watching him as well. In the Sermon on the Mount, Jesus said, "You have heard that it was said, 'Love your neighbor and hate your enemy.' But I tell you: Love your enemies and pray for those who persecute you" (Matthew 5:43–44). This is one of the most profound teachings found anywhere in Scripture, but when Jesus modeled this Scripture in his own life it gained greater meaning for his disciples.

The religious leaders in Jerusalem continually opposed Jesus, yet he never struck back at them. When Jesus was in the Garden of Gethsemane, some soldiers came to arrest him. As those soldiers came to take Jesus away, Peter drew his sword and cut off the ear of one of the high priest's servants. Jesus modeled the teaching of loving his enemy by healing the man's ear (Luke 22:51).

The greatest example of Jesus modeling love for his enemies came as he was hanging on the cross. His enemies had persecuted him, had trumped up charges against him, mocked him, cursed him, and beat him, yet as he hung from the cross, he prayed for them: "Jesus said, 'Father, forgive them, for they do not know what they are doing'" (Luke 23:34). Jesus' life and teaching were one and the same.

Love is at the foundation of the Christian life. As parents make disciples of their children, they must teach them that discipleship is more than rules and regulations. Being a follower of Jesus is about sharing in his ministry. Jesus' ministry was marked by love. Scripture teaches that having spiritual gifts and works without love is empty: "If I speak in the tongues of men and of angels, but have not love, I am only a resounding gong or a clanging cymbal. If I have the gift of prophecy and can fathom all mysteries and all knowledge, and if I have a faith that can move mountains, but have not love, I am nothing. If I give all I possess to the poor and surrender my body to the flames, but have not love, I gain nothing" (1 Corinthians 13:1–3).

When I was a child and would fight with my sister, our grandmother would say, "Why can't we just love one another?" This was her way of paraphrasing the second greatest commandment in all of Scripture: "Love your neighbor as yourself" (Matthew 22:39). Teaching children to love others as themselves means teaching them to treat others the way they would like to be treated (Matthew 7:12). Teaching children to love others as themselves means teaching them to love other children whether they are lovable or not. Often ministry for children will mean reaching out to a child who has been mean or hurtful in the past. Child-sized evangelism includes showing love to one another and loving our neighbors as ourselves.

Mission Projects

There is great value in having your children participate in mission projects. As a pastor I encourage families to be on mission together. I have taken families on mission projects to Romania, Mexico, and various destinations in the United States. Parents who go on a mission with their children help their children to develop a global Christian worldview. Whether children experience missions first-hand or not, missions education should be a part of the discipleship process. Children need to see that there are people in the world who are not like them, yet have the same spiritual, emotional, and physical needs as they do. Mission projects allow children to participate in ministry for their Savior.

Parents do not have to be globetrotters to take their children on a mission. Jesus' commandment to be his witnesses starts in our hometown. For the disciples, missions began in Jerusalem, their hometown, and then expanded to Judea, Samaria, and the ends of the earth (Acts 1:8). Wherever you live there are child-sized mission projects. Parents should look for opportunities to be on mission with their children.

One of my favorite family mission projects was a trip to a church in Matamoras, Mexico. Our mission team did a combination construction and vacation Bible school project. A highlight of the trip was watching the children from our church cross race, language, and culture barriers to express the love of Christ to the people with whom we worked. The families who participated in that project developed a deeper understanding of the call to missions which Jesus places on his followers.

Teach Them to have a Devotional Life

Jesus' disciples can be described as both learners and teachers. As parents learn to follow Jesus, they must also teach their children to follow him. Jesus commanded his disciples to teach new believers to "obey everything I have commanded you" (Matthew 28:20). There is an old saying that actions speak louder than words. Children may hear what we say, but they listen to what we do. Our lives as parents provide a filter for the things we teach our children. It will be hard to teach a child to have a devotional life if the child's parents do not have one of their own. Parents can have the greatest impact on their child's spiritual lives through modeling holy behavior in their own lives.

Devotional Bible Reading

Regular Bible reading is an important part of spiritual growth for Christians of any age. Many parents read from the Bible devotionally each morning or evening, and certainly children will benefit from developing the same spiritual discipline. Just as there are dynamic, contemporary Bible translations geared toward adults, there are many good children's Bibles and children's Bible storybooks on the market as well. Parents can't go wrong in choosing a modern Bible translation for their children written for their reading level. It is exciting when a parent witnesses his or her children reading God's word and hiding it in their young hearts. All three of my children cherish their personal Bibles. Whatever personal devotional Bible reading time a parent may have, their child can participate in a similar activity made to fit their spiritual life and developmental level.

Scripture Memory

The Psalmist described Scripture as "a lamp to my feet and a light for my path" (Psalm 119:105). How true are those words! The Bible guides us, encourages us, equips us to face life, and among many other things is a tool that helps us to worship God. Scripture memory is vital part of the life of a disciple. We need to teach our children to memorize Scripture. Keli and I celebrate with our kids when they memorize Bible verses.

One might think that teaching children to memorize Scripture is a challenge, but that is not the case. I submit that it is easier to teach children to memorize Scripture than it is to teach adults. For years churches and parents have partnered with programs like Bible Drill and Awana Clubs to teach children how to memorize Scripture.

Parents should attempt to make Scripture memory fun, rewarding, and creative. Dads and moms can put Scriptures on flash cards and make a game of memorizing Scripture. The Scriptures on the flash cards can be assigned points and the one who has the most points at the end of the game wins.

Another and more elaborate way to enjoy Scripture memory is to make a board game. Parents and kids can make their own board game by taking a piece of paper and making spaces with a starting line and a finish line. Between start and finish there can be advances and penalties like move ahead two spaces or go back to start. Parents can take flash cards with Scriptures on them and assign a number of spaces according to the difficulty of the Scripture verse. When a verse is right the parent or child can move their game piece the assigned number on the flash card. I know this can be done because my eight-year-old daughter invented such a game herself!

Parents can put sticky notes around the house with Bible verses on them so that the entire home becomes an advertisement for God's word.

In our family we like to make up songs. One of our favorite ways to memorize Scripture is to make up a Scripture song and sing that song. Try singing John 3:16 to the tune of *The Farmer In The Dell*. Use your imagination, and if you have older children, enlist their help to come up with creative rhythms you can set Scripture to.

No matter which method you employ to enable your children to memorize Scripture remember, "all Scripture is God-breathed and is useful for teaching, rebuking, correcting and training in righteousness" (2 Timothy 3:16). Teaching our children to memorize Scripture is one investment that is sure to pay off.

Teach Them to Worship

Our God is a jealous God. He has commanded that his people worship no other gods (Exodus 20:3). Jesus said, "Worship the Lord your God, and serve him only" (Matthew 4:10). Worship is not something limited to adults. As parents we should come to understand that children can worship God too. Not only can children worship God, but he *desires* their worship.

When we worship in front of our children, we will impress upon them the lasting importance of giving honor and glory to a holy, sovereign God. Moses understood the value of this when he directed the Israelites to celebrate the Passover with their children and rehearse over and over again the goodness of God:

> When you enter the land that the LORD will give you as he promised, observe this ceremony. And when your children ask you, "What does this ceremony mean to you?" then tell them, "It is the Passover sacrifice to the LORD, who passed over the houses of the Israelites in Egypt and spared our homes when he struck down the Egyptians." (Exodus 12:25–27)

My paternal grandfather was one of the most rugged men I have ever known. He grew up without a father during the Depression and, as a teenager, survived by farming land for other people. After the Second World

War he bought a farm in Mississippi. Year after year he did the hard work of a farmer. When I was a kid, I used to love to work with him during the summer. One of the most profound memories I have of being with him while he worked is not about the work he was doing. (I think he was mending a fence). What I remember the most was that he was singing an old hymn at the top of his voice. I remember asking him why he was singing so loud. I will never forget what he told me: he was worshipping God! Seeing my grandfather praise God sent a strong and lasting message to a young, impressionable future pastor.

Corporate Worship

When adults think of worship, we often think of what takes place in an organized church, or what can be called *corporate worship*. Children can learn by watching their parents engaged in corporate worship. There is also great value in encouraging children to *participate* in corporate worship themselves. One night while I was at a special performance of our worship choir at church, I kept hearing little voices behind me singing the songs along with the worship choir. I strained to see who it was and saw a group of small children sitting a few rows behind me singing along with the choir. They were engaged in worship every bit as much as, or more than, any adult in the room. I was amazed at their intensity and sincerity. Young children can and do worship.

Parents can help children enjoy and understand worship by working hard to capture the power of the moments in the worship service that are on a child's level. They can review the highlights of the Bible lessons each week with their child and find ways to apply the spiritual truths. They can sing worship songs together and teach that giving is a part of worship. Although some churches offer age-graded worship services for children, parents should still make an effort to reinforce their child's worship experience. Parents should express a deep interest in the Bible memory verses, spiritual truths, video presentations, games, crafts, and dramas used in their worship services.

Family Worship

Family worship time is another great way to teach children about worship. Some families have a daily time of worship where they gather together, read a Bible story, and have prayer. Other families have a weekly time set for worship. Many parents look for special worship opportunities in which to involve their children. Because I am a pastor, my family is extra-involved in church activities; we make a point to look for those special moments around which to center family worship. One example of such a family worship opportunity came after our family had been shopping. We had bought everyone new clothes and had saved a great deal of money. Keli and I gathered the children and had a prayer time of thanksgiving to God for providing our new clothes. One of the most meaningful times of worship for us as a family takes place at Christmas every year. My wife and I work hard to instill in our children that Christmas is about God's greatest gift—not the gifts under the tree.

Families need to worship together. We must instill in our children the understanding that God desires worship from us in every facet of our lives and that it is what we were created for. Families who worship together and share in one another's spiritual lives will find it easier to talk about spiritual matters in times of need. When parents include family worship times in their lives, they teach children to make worship a priority.

Personal Worship

Children can also be taught about the importance of personal worship. What are some things you do in your own individual worship time with God? Now, think about ways to child-size these same worship experiences. One example is journaling. I know some parents who keep a spiritual journal. They write about the prayer requests, blessings, and meaningful spiritual events that have taken place in their own lives. Children can do the same. Parents can encourage their children to write about or draw pictures of the same kinds of things. Moms and dads can then take that child's journal entries and put them in a scrapbook or notebook.

If I could pass just one lesson about worship on to my children, it would be that worship is not just what we *do*; worship is what we *live*. Romans 12:1 says, "Therefore, I urge you, brothers, in view of God's mercy, to offer your bodies as living sacrifices, holy and pleasing to God—this is your spiritual act of worship." Our children can engage in worship when they go to school, when they play, when they pray, and when they learn. Worship can happen when our children win or when they lose. We can teach our children to worship God in the everyday activities of life by helping them to understand that when our lives reflect God, we are worshipping him.

Chapter Ten
God's Plan for Salvation

Yet to all who received him, to those who believed in his name, he gave the right to become children of God. (John 1:12)

Putting the Faith Puzzle Together

LOVE: The First Piece of the Puzzle

Becoming a Christian all starts with love—God's love. The Bible tells us about the love of God.

"This is love: not that we loved God, but that he loved us and sent his Son as an atoning sacrifice for our sins" (1 John 4:10).

"But God demonstrates his own love for us in this: While we were still sinners, Christ died for us" (Romans 5:8)

God loves _____ (*Write your name in the blank.*) He has created you, and he has a special plan for your life.

SIN: The Second Piece of the Puzzle

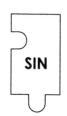

God loves us and wants to have a relationship with us, but there is a problem. That problem is called sin. Sin is a rebellious heart attitude that leads us to say or think or do things that God does not want us to do. Sin separates us from God. The Bible tells us about sin.

"But your iniquities have separated you from your God; your sins have hidden his face from you, so that he will not hear" (Isaiah 59:2). Circle the word that means sin (*iniquities*). God really wants to be in our lives, but sin separates us from him.

"For the wages of sin is death" (Romans 6:23). Sin separates us from God and brings spiritual death into our lives. This verse means that because of our sins we cannot go to be with God in heaven.

"For all have sinned and fall short of the glory of God" (Romans 3:23). Circle the word *all*. Everyone has sinned.

Can you think of some things you have said, thought, or done that God did not want you to do?

_____

_____

_____

JESUS: The Third Piece of the Puzzle

God sent his son, Jesus, to die on the cross for you so that he can have a relationship with you and give you spiritual life. We can be forgiven for our sins, have a relationship with him, and one day go to heaven because of what Jesus has done for us. The Bible talks about Jesus Christ.

"For Christ died for sins once for all, the righteous for the unrighteous, to bring you to God" (1 Peter 3:18). Circle the phrase *Christ died for sins* in this verse.

God loves us so much that he sent his son Jesus to the cross to die in our place and bring us to God. Do you believe Jesus died on the cross for your sins so that you can be forgiven of your sins and have a relationship with him? _____

FAITH: The Fourth Piece of the Puzzle

Jesus died on the cross for us and rose up from the grave. If we have faith in Jesus and ask him to forgive our sins, he will come into our lives and make us God's children. The Bible talks about faith.

"Yet to all who received him, to those who believed in his name, he gave the right to become children of God" (John 1:12). We are not saved by anything we do, but by God's gift of his son Jesus. All God asks us to do is to believe in Jesus and confess our faith in him as our Lord.

"For if you confess with your mouth that Jesus is Lord and believe in your heart that God raised him from the dead, you will be saved. For it is by believing in your heart that you are made right with God, and it is by confessing with your mouth that you are saved. As the Scriptures tell us, 'Anyone who believes in him will not be disappointed'" (Romans 10:9–11 NLT). Circle the words *confess* and *confessing* in these Bible verses.

The word confess means to admit something out loud. What does God want us to confess? _____

_____

Are you ready to become a Christian by confessing your faith in Jesus? _____

LOVE

Becoming a Christian starts with God's love. The Bible tells us about the love of God.

- "This is love: not that we loved God, but that he loved us and sent his Son as an atoning sacrifice for our sins" (1 John 4:10).

- "But God demonstrates his own love for us in this: While we were still sinners, Christ died for us" (Romans 5:8).

SIN

The Bible tells us that we have all sinned. None of us have always perfectly done what God wants us to do.

- "For all have sinned and fall short of the glory of God" (Romans 3:23).

- "For the wages of sin is death" (Romans 6:23). The Bible tells us that sin brings death into our lives. Sin separates us from God.

JESUS

God sent his son Jesus to die on the cross for you so that you can have forgiveness for sin and eternal life. We can go to heaven one day because of what Jesus has done for us.

- "For Christ died for sins once for all, the righteous for the unrighteous, to bring you to God" (1 Peter 3:18). God loves us so much that he sent his son Jesus to the cross to die in our place and bring us to God.

FAITH

If we believe in Jesus Christ and ask him to come into our lives he will make us God's children.

- "Yet to all who received him to those who believed in his name, he gave the right to become children of God" (John 1:12).

- "For if you confess with your mouth that Jesus is Lord and believe in your heart that God raised him from the dead you will be saved" (Romans 10:9).

Putting All the Pieces Together

How to Become a Christian

If you are ready to become a Christian, then it is time to pray and tell God what you believe about Jesus. The Bible tells us, "Everyone who calls on the name of the Lord will be saved" (Romans 10:13).

We call on God through prayer. As we pray there are some things we need to tell him.

We need to tell God that we know he loves us.

We need to admit that we have sinned and we need forgiveness.

We need to confess that we believe in Jesus and that we want him to be our Lord.

You can pray your own prayer that includes these things or you can pray a prayer like this one:

Dear God,

Thank you for loving me. I know that I have sinned and that my sin separates me from you. Please forgive me. I believe Jesus died on the cross for my sins and that he is alive today. Jesus, please come into my heart to be my Lord and Savior. I want to live for you for the rest of my life. Thank you for saving me and giving me eternal life. Amen.

What Now?

Welcome to the family of God. If you have prayed that prayer and meant it with all of your heart, then you are now one of God's children. Now that you are one of his children, there are several things you will need to do.

Tell some of the people you love that you have become a Christian.

If you have a pastor, Sunday school teacher, or children's minister, tell them the good news.

Read your Bible so that you will know God's plan for your life and so that you will know how to become an obedient disciple of Jesus.

Pray. Prayer is talking to God. Now that you are one of his children, you will want to talk to him as often as possible about everything in your life.

Will God Always Love You?

When we invite Jesus into our heart, we become one of God's children. We will always be his children just like you will always be your parent's child. The Bible tells us that nothing can separate us from the love of God that we have in Jesus (Romans 8:39). God loved you even before you loved him (Romans 5:8). God will always love you.

What If You Sin?

You *will* sin again, but your sins are now forgiven. When we sin we hurt those we sin against, like our friends and our family. Sin hurts us as well. But, worst of all, sin hurts our heavenly Father who loved us so much that he gave his son, Jesus, to die on the cross for those sins. So we must try our hardest to live like God wants us to live. But when we do sin, God wants us to ask him for forgiveness. 1 John 1:9 tells us how God forgives his children, "If we confess our sins, he is faithful and just to forgive us our sins, and to cleanse us from all unrighteousness" (1 John 1:9 KJV). When we do sin, all we have to do is to admit to God how we have sinned and ask him to forgive us of that sin. We have his promise in the Bible that he will forgive us.

What If You Do Not *Feel* like God's Child?

There will be times in your life when you may not feel close to God. All Christians will have times like this in our lives. Sometimes we will feel happy, and sometimes we will feel sad. We will get angry, and there will be times when we will be bored. There will even be times when we don't feel like going to church. Our relationship to God is not based on a feeling. I am glad about this because my feelings change a lot. From the Bible we learn that our relationship to God is not based on anything we feel or do: "God saved you by his special favor when you believed. And you can't take credit for this; it is a gift from God. Salvation is not a reward for the good things we have done, so none of us can boast about it" (Ephesians 2:8–9 NLT).

Appendix A

This certificate is also available to download from
www.authenticbooks.com/documents/ctm_certificate.pdf

Certificate of Commitment

Made a faith commitment

to Jesus Christ as Lord and Savior on

Pastor

Proud Parent

Appendix B
Read-Along Bible Story Books for Children

Davidson, Alice J. *The Story of Jonah.* Norwalk: C. R. Gibson Company, 1984.

Fries, Tess. *Moses: Baby in the Bulrushes.* Franklin, TN: Dalmatian Press, 2001.

Fries, Tess. *Joseph and His Coat of Many Colors.* Franklin, TN: Dalmatian Press, 2001.

Fries, Tess. *Adam and Eve.* Franklin, TN: Dalmatian Press, 2001.

Keefer, Lois and Susan Martins. *Family Fun Stuff Bible Stories (Elementary).* Colorado Springs: Cook Communications Ministries, 2001.

Ladwig, Tim. *Psalm Twenty-Three.* Grand Rapids: Eerdmans Books for Young Readers, 1997.

Morgan, Robert J. *The Children's Daily Devotional Bible.* Nashville: Thomas Nelson, 1996.

Nathan-Deiller, Muriel. *The Greatest Stories Ever Told.* Nashville: Broadman and Holman Publishers, 1998.

Pingry, Patricia A. *The Story of the Ten Commandments.* Nashville: Ideals Publications, 1999.

Wildsmith, Brian. *Exodus.* Grand Rapids, MI: Eerdmans Books for Young Readers, 1999.

Wildsmith, Brian. *Jesus.* Grand Rapids: Eerdmans Books for Young Readers, 2000.

Yenne, Bill. *The Story of the First Easter.* Nashville: Thomas Nelson, 1994.

Appendix C

Values-Based Children's Video Series

The following list is just a sampling of the many wonderful children's video series that are now available for parents to use to teach spiritual values to their children.

Adventures in Odyssey. Fast-paced family adventure by Focus On The Family. Nashville: Tommy Nelson.

The Beginners Bible. Animated versions of favorite Bible stories. New York: Sony Wonder.

The Bible Man Adventures. Action, music, light-hearted humor, and adventure with Christian values. Portland: Pamplin Entertainment.

The Crippled Lamb and *Jacob's Gift.* Videos based on books by Max Lucado. Nashville: Thomas Nelson.

Mr. Henry's Wild and Wacky Bible Stories. Humor, music, and important lessons about God and His Word by author Frank Peretti. Nashville: Tommy Nelson.

VeggieTales. Values-based family media products produced by Big Idea Productions, Lombard, Illinois.